WONDER

The Breathless Adventure of Chasing The Heart of God

Michael W. Thompson

Revival Life Press

Library of Congress Cataloging-in-Publication Data: An application to register this book for cataloging has been submitted to the Library of Congress.
Paperback ISBN: 9798429803722
Paperback and E-Book, First Edition: March 2022

Author's website: www.MichaelWThompson.com

DEDICATION

To Bill Johnson, my visionary friend who from a distance, mentored me in the joy and reality of Kingdom *"on earth as it is in Heaven."*

Your love saw beyond my failure, your faith believed more than most saw and your hope helped reignite passion in my worn and weary soul. It would be impossible to overstate what you have taught Dianne and me.

Your invitation for me to return after 25 years and speak at Bethel prompted the message that underscores this book. The visit and ministry there among such people of wonder confirmed its message and its value to other wonder-walkers.

We will be forever grateful for the example you and Beni display of a life lived in wonder.

> *"I'll make up for the years of the locust...You'll eat your fill*
> *of good food. You'll be full of praises to your God,*
> ***The God who has set you back on your heels in wonder."***
>
> (Joel 2:25-26, MSG)

TABLE OF CONTENTS

PREFACE

Wonder.

A single word describes the atmosphere and defines the attitude that underwrites the adventure of chasing Jesus.

Wonder sees God's heart as an underground cavern labyrinth with more twists and turns, more places to discover, more surprises to unearth, than we could ever imagine. Best of all, He invites us to explore freely and experience fully the depths of that heart.

God opens His wonders to anyone who chooses wonder.

An obsession with wonder possessed my heart through an odd flow of events. It started with an email. This message took me quite by surprise because of the unexpected invitation it contained. The kindness it reflected took my breath away as I read it in my lounge chair that April evening.

Tears came without warning. Wonder rode in their wake.

This was an invitation to return after 25 years and speak at Bethel Church in Redding, California. That might not seem all that striking to you, but to me, it was like a posted notice releasing me from a cave that had confined me for over two decades.

Let me fill in the blanks with some backstory.

Bethel was a house that not only had been a highlight of our ministry during that season so many years prior, but in the succeeding years had contributed massively to our healing and restoration. Not long after that first visit to Bethel, many years of externally successful ministry imploded as I royally crashed and burned. Life as I'd known it disintegrated. Thus began my backside of the desert experience.

God made himself known in healing, grace and favor while my whole family wandered in that arid space. We discovered things about Him and His love that we would never have known without those dire days. Jesus became more real than we'd ever dreamed; Holy Spirit closer than we'd ever imagined.

1

Just happy to be alive and restored, we never imagined that God still had a place for us to serve and give. Out of sheer gratitude for grace, we put our hands to any small task Jesus put before us. Slowly, the flower of our faith unfolded its petals again. Hope appeared like a rainbow after a storm.

The email from my friend Bill Johnson seemed a message from God that went something like this.

> "You've walked in tough places, learned hard lessons, changed intractable behaviors, found incredible release and discovered the beauty of my presence. You're now astonished at my goodness and amazed by my grace. My ability to turn the worst situations into Kingdom gold has left you in awe. You've become a wonder-walker. So go tell my people what it's like to live in that wonder."

It was nearly nine months after the email that I stood in Bethel's pulpit and poured out the message that birthed this book. Gestation started the day after I received that momentous email. You hold the baby in your hands.

God dropped the essence of this word into my heart almost as soon as I read the invitation. By the time I spoke the message, this book was nearing completion. My heart for you is that these pages infect you with a sense of awe so deep and so profound that even the most mundane moments of your daily are lit up with His presence and purpose.

Wonder describes both the change in my life and what changed my life. Childlike fascination with Jesus is transforming my experience of Him and how I chase Him with my life. Little wonder I am obsessed with this theme.

Let these words guide you into a space where you live the breathless adventure of chasing God's heart. Slip the surly bonds of secularized gravity and take wing on the wind of the Spirit. Discover what it means to have Jesus take your breath away and leave you speechless. Let Him thrill you again.

Your life can still sing a song of joy, no matter what you've been through.

Wonder works!

Your understanding of me brings me wonder and strength.
~Psalm 139:5-6

JET LAGGED

"Sometimes you have to go up really high
to understand how small you are."
~Felix Baumgartner

At only six, the little boy forever changed my experience of flight.

I spend a lot of time on planes. Over 20 years of travel for my work racked up 80-100,000 domestic air miles each year. Two things happen when you fly that much: you gain all the perks of the airline you fly; and you grow completely numb to the experience of flying.

A few years back, a little boy turned off my autopilot and put the miracle back into the friendly skies. That single flight leg renewed both my heart and mind.

We veteran flyers boarded early and flopped into our upgraded seats, prepared to slap on noise-canceling headphones, fire up tablets and hibernate for four hours. That's when it started. Sitting next to his dad just across the aisle from me, this young boy simply couldn't believe his eyes and he wouldn't stop talking about it.

With breathless enthusiasm, he offered a 30-minute non-stop, play-by-play color commentary of all the amazing stuff he'd never seen before. No one in the cabin seemed to mind too much. After all, he wasn't a hardened frequent flyer like the rest of us. It was his first time on a plane.

The dead giveaway was, he looked out the window. He saw what the rest of us took for granted because we'd seen it a thousand times before. As this boy described to his father everything he saw, the rest of us got to hear the magic his unschooled, neophyte eyes observed.

It was quite simply, magical.

"Daddy, daddy…there are guys down there with shiny vests on…what do you think they're doing? Oh man, there's some kind of really cool truck…it has a big ramp on it…they're putting it against the plane…whoa, Dad, suitcases are going up the ramp…you think I can see our suitcases?"

Thus started the exciting narrative of the ground crew. The mood in the cabin lightened with amusement. In the stagnate, artificially filtered atmosphere of that plane, this was a deep breath of fresh air. The intensity of his story-telling amped up as we backed away from the gate.

"Dad…we're moving…we're backing up…wow, some guys out there are waving red light thingies…hey, Dad, we're going forward now…feels like we are going faster…look daddy, look! We're going up…we're leaving the ground. Dad, we're flying!!!!"

Now imagination was in overdrive. "Dad, you won't believe it… the cars are getting smaller…they look like my hot wheels…the buildings too…just like my Legos…" He nearly exploded as we slipped into the cumulus cover blanketing the sky.

"Hey daddy, there's white stuff out the window…what's the white stuff dad?" The young father barely got the words "those are clouds" out of his mouth before the boy shouted, "Clouds!" Are we up in the clouds? No way!…they look like marshmallows. I think I could eat them!"

We broke through the cloud deck and it was a moment I will never forget. "Dad, Dad, Hey Dad! I SEE THE SUN!!"

This was the breathless commentary of a heart experiencing for the very first time the overwhelming joy of flight. His were the animated expressions of a kid on a big, breathless adventure, seeing marvelous things. Things so commonplace for his grizzled traveling companions they'd become invisible. Cushy first-class seats left us anesthetized. Dead to what made his little heart race. To his untutored eyes, every detail was exceptional, every moment extraordinary.

To us weary road warriors, his prattling on could have been annoying. But that day it was endearing. We sat captivated. The entire section was soon laughing, vicariously experiencing the same novel excitement enrapturing the little fella. Seeing through his unclouded eyes transported us back to our first time on a plane. We sat astonished. We entered his wonder.

His wonder made that flight wonder-full for the rest of us.

As weary travelers, we focused solely on one goal: destination. Our little friend was lost in a different reality: journey. For the rest of that long flight, we all got lost with him. His dumbstruck fascination shifted the atmosphere for we who were tired of travel.

I watched for the rest of the flight as people chatted freely with each other. Headsets stayed on laps. Tablets remained off. Laughter filled the cabin. People were connecting, enjoying a routine suddenly filled with life again. That little boy let loose a contagion—a virus that infected everyone hearing him.

It's called *Wonder*.

Here's what struck me so deeply that day. He was looking out the same windows as everyone else but seeing something altogether different. The rest of us should have seen things just like that little guy. But we didn't. What was taking his breath away was putting us to sleep.

The difference? We had been there, done that and had drawers full of the T-shirts to prove it. All we heard was white noise numbing our crowded minds and weary hearts. There was simply nothing left to sweep us off our feet.

Our problem was we knew it all

We often live too much life in a perpetual state of jet lag. Eager for the destination, weary on the journey. We miss so much beauty around us because we lose wonder within us. Trapped in routines, numbed by redundancy, we get discouraged by miles traveled but destinations unreached. Dull disenchantment with the *now* becomes the norm.

The plane ride with that little boy began a process of renewal in my heart and mind. As quick as a thought, I can be back in that plane cabin again, touched by the wonder of that moment. It reverberates in my heart to this day because it became a core reality that now serves as the single key to my personal revival. It's so simple.

I am made for wonder.

You are too.

TURBULENCE

"To fly, we have to have resistance.
It's all about turbulence."
~Maya Lin

God made us for "WOW!"

Like the kid on my flight, we're meant to travel breathlessly, discover passionately and adventure endlessly. He designed each of us to live an *"I-can't-even-believe-it"* life. I know it sounds silly when it feels like life yanked the rug from under you and planted you face first in a tackle box. None-the-less, God intended for us to pursue Heaven for all we're worth.

David unearthed this wisdom smack in the middle of a life filled with more questions than answers and more trouble than most people ever see. He uncovered eternal hope in the daily grind.

He sums it up like this: *"I am fearfully and wonderfully made."* [1]

The Hebrew word translated *"fearfully"* means awe, reverence or honor. *"Wonderfully"* describes distinctiveness—"one-of-a-kind-ness." God intricately formed every human being with a blow-your-mind, leave-you-scratching-your-head uniqueness. When any human walks into any room—if correctly understood—it should suck the oxygen out of the place. Why? Because they have the design of God behind them and the image of God within them.

Thinking about it caused David to declare, *"Everything you do is marvelously breathtaking. It simply amazes me to think about it!"* [2]

God is a God of wonders. That automatically makes us people of wonder. Wonder is our natural environment, just as worship is our native tongue.

"Lord, you are great and worthy of the highest praise! For there is no end to the discovery of the greatness that surrounds you. Generation after generation will declare more of your greatness and declare more of your glory."[3.]

If my assumption is correct, then it is vital to understand what I mean by "wonder."

Wonder is the I-can't-catch-my-breath approach to God's presence, power and provision. It is the only honest, logical reaction to who God is and what He's done. Wonder is the natural response to the nearness—the hereness—of the King and His Kingdom. Wonder sees Kingdom all the time, everywhere.

When you truly grasp the meaning Jesus pours into the most banal routines, it grabs you by the throat and shakes you awake. In the Kingdom of God, to see the mundane as profane is insane!

Wonder is the CSI approach to life in God

When we live in wonder, we are constantly dusting the tough spaces of life for fingerprints. God's fingerprints. The forensic evidence that He has been in this place and left me hints of His presence. We waken to the eternal detail and divine texture within the ordinary. We pay adorational attention to His presence hiding in the every-day-ness of living.

I've discovered that if I see His fingerprints, I want to see His hand. When I see His hand, I long to seek His face. When I see His face, I'm propelled into wonder.

Finding a hint of His hidden presence in any area of my life creates desire to experience His manifest presence in every arena of my life. The subtle scent of His presence creates a longing for the full aroma of His person.

Please don't make the mistake of believing this wonder is some ethereal, out-of-touch-with-how-it-is spiritual smokescreen. This idea doesn't come from the shallowness of a sheltered life unfamiliar with genuine struggle and tragedy. I've mined the treasures of wonder the old-fashioned way—through a lot of dirt and darkness.

I've seen the incapacitating distress of:

- An ongoing, debilitating disease that cost me a sizeable portion of my digestive system in an agonizing, life-altering surgery.
- A mother caught in the constricting trap of dementia where Alzheimer's stole her golden years, leaving her unable to recall my name during her last decade.
- A personal failure so catastrophic that I imploded my life, left my family a pile of ashes. alienated close friends and destroyed everything for which I worked.

So understand, I do not see wonder as some pie-in-the-sky panacea; some trivial faith-fantasy fairy tale. Not at all. Wonder isn't some mushy mindset that fiddles while Rome burns. In fact, Jesus is more present to our harsh reality than we are.

I get that *life-as-it-is* can knock the stuffing out of *life-as-it-should-be*. Pain colors our glasses with shades of skepticism and shadows of cynicism until nothing in life looks clear, crisp or bright anymore.

The incredible power of wonder is that it takes a militant stance against the apathy and agony of the surrounding darkness. It believes there is destiny behind every tragedy, meaning beyond every mystery.

Wonder walks on water in the worst storms

This wonder is authentic to the rub and reality of a world gone mad. But it simply refuses to let go of the unshakeable truth that God is good and the evidence of His goodness is all over life.

The wonder I'm talking about is a...

- Full-throated confession that no matter what is happening, all things work together for good—so *"in everything,"* I can truly *"give thanks."*[4]
- Full-blown acceptance that despite how little I understand, the plans God has for me are right—so in it all I can *"rejoice with joy unspeakable and full of glory."*[5]
- Full-scale declaration that in the face of incalculable odds, nothing can separate me from the love of God—so I can confidently *"rejoice in the Lord always."*[6]

- Full-on expectation that even though I feel alone, He will never leave or forsake me—so I can *"forget what is behind and press on to the high calling of God in Christ Jesus."*[7]

Wonder steels us for the worst life throws at us because it understands there is so much we just don't know. So much stuff that is out-of-bounds and above our heads about which we have no clue. It flies in the face of artificial assurance that "everything will turn out right." Instead, wonder grasps that everything will be alright no matter how it turns out, because we have a good Father.

Truth is, if life has no mystery, it has no wonder.

Kingdom mindset is comfortable with mystery. It grows accustomed to embracing a life with far more unanswered questions than unquestioned answers.

Wonder simply refuses to fret over the wrong questions. Instead, it's captivated by the One who knows all the stuff we'll never figure out. We live aware that we can only deal with the past by repentance and forgiveness. The future is the sole domain of hope.

Wonder walks present to the present. It is alive to and aware of the now presence of Jesus in the now realities of life. No matter the fog of mystery shrouding my life, there is someone doing something more than I can see or comprehend.

The smartest man in history said it this way, *"Don't think for a moment that you know it all, for wisdom comes when you adore him with undivided devotion."*[8] There is constant discovery when we live with curiosity at full tilt and imagination full speed ahead.

Wonder is a lifestyle of Divine surprise.

Jeremiah was an Old Testament prophet rocked by tragedy, shaken by doubts and crushed by disappointments. It is to him in the heart of those difficulties that God said, *"Call to Me, and I will answer you, and show you great and mighty things, **which you do not know.**"*[9]

God was revealing a profound truth that is cornerstone and capstone to a renewed mind.

There is incredible supernatural power in not knowing it all!

Now this mindset is not for the faint of heart. Life as we live it often robs us of wonder. Living gets all up in your face with the pace of its demands. We exist under perpetual pressure—busy, frazzled, weighed down, discouraged, frustrated, disillusioned.

It's so easy to become captive to living instead of captivated by life.

Sometimes it's all you can do to grab a second to think about God, much less slow down and get lost in wonder. The stress of "adulting" steals the aura of freshness and splendor that should characterize following Jesus. Randall Worley notes, "We have become sleepwalkers in a world of absolute wonder. We ask for the supposed invisible God to reveal himself and forget that He is everywhere."

Church as we know it can deflate wonder just as quickly. Religious folk often relegate wonder to moments—transitory events, fleeting encounters, "aha" experiences. While these clock-stopping, heart-racing instances are great and remind us of the awe in which we ought always to live, they often fade as quickly as they come. Small moments can have a big impact, but they are still only moments.

Reflecting on the weariness, complacency and frustration of doing church without awe grieves me. God never intended for the Bride of Jesus to wear rags of shame or live in hovels of hypocrisy. If we not only accept as normal but elevate as holy, living with less than His intention for us, it is no wonder there is no wonder!

Maybe what we are after, what we really need, is a revival of wonder. A rebirth of amazement, a resurrection of awe, a renovation of imagination. Something deeply spiritual with a long shelf-life and no expiration date.

Isn't that what we mean when we pray Jesus' words *"on earth as it is in heaven?"* The intricate connection between everything of us we now see and everything of Jesus we have not yet seen.

Jesus called it His Kingdom of Heaven. In that Kingdom, wonder is the way of life.

A CHILD'S-EYE VIEW

"If we experienced life through the eyes of a child,
everything would be magical and extraordinary."
~ Akiane Kramarik

Isaiah once predicted: *"For unto us a child is born unto us a son is given...and His name shall be called Wonderful..."*[1] There is actually no word in Hebrew that we can correctly translate *"wonderful."* The text actually reads, *"His name shall be called WONDER."*

Breathtaking wonder is as organic to the Kingdom as the King's name.

Jesus said His Kingdom is always *"at hand"*[2]—so close we can touch it. Yet, that Realm is so beyond, so big, so baffling that to live in it is to live with more questions than answers.

We humans want certainty. God loves curiosity. We ache for sure-footed stances. God gets a kick out of watching us slide on the ice. We love to march our ducks in precise rows. God's Dove delights flying in circles.

Rabbi Jesus took just such an unsettling approach with His disciples all the time. Gospel writers frequently record the crowds who didn't really know Jesus being amazed at Him. But they also report how the friends of Jesus, who lived with him 24-7-365 and to whom he was constantly explaining all the stuff He said and did, were awestruck too. They scratched their heads more than anyone.

No teaching of Jesus was more jarring than when He stood a little kid before these would-be leaders and said, *"Truly I say to you, whoever does not receive the kingdom of God like a child will not enter it at all."*[3] He was saying, "If you don't grasp it like a child, you won't get it at all. If you don't wonder at it, you'll never walk in it."

This whole discussion raises a profound theological question for me: Why do we stop skipping?

Skipping characterizes Children. Walking marks adults. Or worse, plodding. When does that change? Why does it change? Jesus flatly states that we must get the skip back in our steps if we want to travel in the Kingdom. G. K. Chesterton once said, "The true object of all human life is play."[4] I think Jesus agreed.

We must *"change (repent) and become like a child,"*[5] He says. This means start seeing "what is" through the eyes of "what can be." My little clueless friend on the plane that day saw things in a different light than the rest of us who felt we *knew* what was going on.

Jesus' directives are clear.

- *REPENT*—for what you've made of yourself. You have forgotten how to pay attention. Change your mind so God can shape you for all you're worth.
- *RETURN*—to how God made you. He created you to live in awestruck amazement of your Father and His world. Change your mind so you can see God for all He's worth.

Children have an uncanny capacity to marvel over even the smallest things. Ordinary captivates them. Wonder creates the same awe in our minds and hearts. It keeps us at spiritual attention. We live with dreams on fire again. That is the essence of the childlike heart.

> *The most defining trait of childlikeness is imagination*

Sacred imagination alone is the characteristic that keeps us focused on His face, attentive to His every move and responsive to His heartbeat. Fascination with Him is the single most powerful weapon against the insipid and insidious allure of the surrounding culture. Only infatuation with something higher will keep us from succumbing to the pull of lesser affections.

14

That's how wonder works.

But there's more. Wonder is cyclical. Our wonder inspires God to do wonders, while God's doing wonders generates more wonder. Nothing is better than getting caught in that vortex.

David's life was replete with disappointment, failure, frustration, injustice and loss. But right in the middle of it, he rediscovered the power of wonder. One day, he looked in the mirror at the same old face but saw something different. It catapulted him into a place of awe, overwhelmed by the One who created him.

He heard music—the song of God over His life. He realized he was God's opus.

It snatched David's breath away to realize, *"You have searched me, Lord, and you know me."*[6] Brian Simmons renders it this way in the Passion Translation, *"Lord, you know everything there is to know about me."* David was gobsmacked that God was intimately familiar with every square inch of his life. Nothing in the sphere of David's identity was outside the orbit of the Father's concern.

Reflecting on David's awakening has awakened something in me. I now understand something that before I only speculated about. To see the amazing wonder of God requires a specific lens.

My life is that lens. So is yours.

David's encounter became the heart of his familiar sonnet, Psalm 139. Let's do a deep dive into this incredible song. We'll unpack the four key Discoveries that reignited wonder in the old Hymnist's heart.

Perhaps it will light the same fire in us.

DISCOVERY

God Is Writing My Story

From Once Upon A Time

To Happily Ever After

Psalm 139:2-4

You know when I sit and when I rise; you perceive my thoughts from afar. You discern my going out and my lying down; you are familiar with all my ways. Before a word is on my tongue you, Lord, know it completely.

AUTHORIZED BIOGRAPHY

"Biography is the only true history."
~ Thomas Carlyle

She came to the well at a time no one else did because hers was a sad story of bad choices and broken relationships. He was such a scoundrel he climbed a tree to avoid the crowd since his was a wicked tale of fraud and deceit. Her defiled hands poured perfume on His holy feet, just one more risk in an ongoing drama of shattered promises and desperate love.

Their approach was timid and distant; they were embarrassed and ashamed. Each one living a tragedy of sick bodies and broken hearts.

"Unworthy" etched his face like a birthmark. This soldier, with a dark backstory of violence and control, dared not even invite help into his home.

Life was a matrix of self-pity and self-loathing for this man, an autobiography of disappointment with God and people.

> *"You have searched me, Lord, and you know me."*
>
> *~Psalm 139:1*

All true stories of life on a broken planet. People whose day-to-day was a carousel of pain, rejection, depletion and sorrow. Walking wounded—more accurately, the walking dead. These anonymous snippets are only a few of the painful dramas that intersected with Jesus during His three-year crash course on the Kingdom. Their sagas represent sad stories repeated every day all around us.

Fact is, everybody has a story. Whoever you run into as you walk through today has a very personal backstory.

- Every homeless person on the street.
- That uniquely complicated guy at work.
- The checkout lady, mechanic, server, nurse or pilot.
- Each troubled teen, stressed spouse or lonely grandparent.

Everyone has a story. It is the bane of our modern cancel culture that we crudely condense perplexing life stories with a label.

It happened all the time in the Bible[1].

- *The demoniac* of Gadara.
- A woman with an *issue of blood*.
- *Blind* Bartimaeus.
- Simon *the leper*.
- A man with *the withered hand*.

We find it far too easy to minimize complex biographies through the inherent arrogance of labeling. Happens every day: the divorcee, the unfaithful spouse, the addict, the teen mom, the loser dad, the religious freak, the crooked boss, the lazy employee, the fallen leader. Slap a label on someone and you think you capture the story.

Labels never tell the whole truth

Yes, everyone has a story. Take it a step further. Everyone *IS* a story…and the end is not yet written. It's too easy to forget this essential reality. We can't afford to overlook or dismiss the biographies of those we meet—no matter how beautiful or painful the plot.

Every one of those stories matters to God. God never reads or writes labels. He is always concerned with the complete story. He is a master at taking the worst stories and making them wonder-full.

David realized this as he looked at himself in the mirror. *"Like an open book, you watched me grow from conception to birth; all the stages of my life were spread out before you, the days of my life all prepared before I'd even lived one day."*[2]

God alone knew *the whole story*. He was the only Author who could accurately write the details. Understanding God's role as the author of his life changed David's perspective on everything he experienced—good and bad.

The Lord knew the end from the beginning. Nothing took Him by surprise. My spiritual papa, Jack Taylor, used to quip, "it occurred to me that nothing ever occurred to God." Everything that came into David's life had to first pass through the lens of God's vision for Him. The Creator was the Psalmist's *authorized* biographer.

David got that. Sometimes we don't.

We lose wonder when we allow other authors to scribe our stories. I realize there may be contributors who lend a hand filling out the plot along the way, but no ghostwriter will get the story right. Even your best friends see only the chapter you're in. If you let anyone make the chapter you're living all there is to the story, you'll stop in the messy middle and miss the epic ending.

> *You can't get the ending right*
> *if you tell the story wrong*

If we allow other people to pen their fiction into our plot, the narrative gets stuck in a sidebar. You must never allow the moral of your story to be shifted by pain, failure, people or culture.

- If you tell yourself the wrong story about you.
  you'll end up being a lie.
- If you embrace the wrong story about someone else.
  you'll end up believing a lie.

David embraced the naked truth that God *searched* him. God *got* him. The Almighty knew him because He made him. In the Divine searching, God ferreted out what needed to be harmonized to the original storyline. Yahweh knew the intricacies of the story from prologue to epilogue, so the chapters were always congruent to an ending already written.

So the question for us is, *Who is writing your story?*

Is there a collaborative—a gaggle of people whose opinions are shaping your life-plot? Or is there One Author? An eternal biographer who has complete editorial control of the storyline. You are being authored. Either by a collective of authors imposing their editorial view on your life, or by *"the Author and Finisher of your faith."*[3]

If He's the author, He's in charge of the storyline. If He's the finisher, He controls the ending. Wonder happens in the middle!

Peter once referred to Jesus as *"the Author of life,"*[4] Paul said, *"You are a letter from Christ...written not with ink but with the Spirit of the living God, not on tablets of stone but on tablets of human hearts."*[5] Each of us has the potential to be a biography God writes.

Don't disqualify yourself because of chapters in life you wish no one could read. Ugliness in your backstory is as a stark backdrop against which God displays the beauty of the story. And His stories always have the best endings.

Jesus always writes "Godographies!"

We maximize our sense of wonder when we embrace that the God who writes our stories never runs out of plot twists or alternate endings! I am awestruck reading His work in my life as He weaves the story into a plot I would never dare to believe. How could God do such a thing with "lil ol' me?" How could He rework the tragedies, mistakes, failures and pain of my life into a story that declares beautifully who He is and what He is like?

Truly, this is *amazing* grace!

We dare not edit the stories of people around us either. We don't know how their story is supposed to end. If we forget people have backstories or treat any chapter like it is the complete story, we lose compassion, break connection and create condemnation. As followers of Jesus, above all other voices in society, we should champion their stories.

We understand God by how He acted and acts in relation to His people. My heart swells at the picture of God I see in the lives of those I love. As they struggle to follow the divine narrative, I see hints of who He is.

It simply takes my breath away.

There's an even greater reality to all this. God knits together the collection of our life stories and turns them into history—*His*-story.

The span of Scripture unveils *the story of God* through the collected stories of His people. The Bible is a narrative of individual testimonies woven into a tapestry called Kingdom.

Telling our stories creates the ongoing narrative of the Kingdom. We radicalize relationships when we share stories.

The power of testimony is half the reason we win in the end. *"They triumphed over him by the blood of the Lamb and by **the word of their testimony**."*[6] The testimony of Jesus, which becomes the word of prophecy,[7] declares loudly over my life that what God did for them, He can do for me.

We must never stop sharing our stories. The atmosphere of wonder increases, spreads and deepens as we swap stories.

BETWEEN THE
LINES

> "Yet the deepest truths are best read between the lines, and,
> for the most part, refuse to be written."
> ~ *Amos Bronson Alcott*

Every life is a narrative written by hand—either the hand of unsettling circumstance or the hand of the unshakeable God. Giving the pen to the right author determines which story gets told.

That's what underscores this incredible verse: *"Give thanks to the Lord, for he is good; his love endures forever.* **Let the redeemed of the Lord tell their story**—*those he redeemed from the hand of the foe, those he gathered from the lands, from east and west, from north and south."*[1]

> "You know when I sit and when I rise; you perceive my thoughts from afar."
>
> ~Psalm 139:2

The Psalmist knows that in your life, the impact of your story rises from the way God reframes your failures and recasts your pain. You have been redeemed! That is a story worth telling. There's such wonder in that narrative.

The power of story comes from the wisdom of the writer. Too often, the moral of our story gets devalued because of all our errors. But the tales of the Kingdom are fraught with broken lives, broken hearts and broken promises.

David emphatically states that while we may have trouble reading between the lines, God has never had a problem writing between them.

Look at the stories this Psalmist said the redeemed should tell (Psalm 107).

- **Wanderers**. *"Some wandered"* and became nomads in wastelands. They got lost, got hungry and got desperate. In despair, they cried out to God and He led them home. The song instructs them to celebrate their stories because of the God who revealed his goodness and mercy through them (vv 4-9).
- **Prisoners**. *"Some sat in darkness"* imprisoned by chains forged by their own hands. Penal work was hard. Their strength grew feeble. But in His mercy, God broke their bonds and set them free. To these ex-cons, the Psalmist commends joyful singing because God rewrote the end of their stories (vv 10-16).
- **Rebels**. *"Some became fools"* because they decided they could out-think God. Through their own rebellion, fighting against the very God who wanted nothing but good for them, they ended up sick to death of life. Ready to give up. Yet when they simply called on God, He sent His word and healed them. Songs of celebration and offerings of thanksgiving were the natural response the Psalmist dictated (vv 17-22).
- **Runners**. *"Others went out on the sea"* running from the plan and purpose of the One who made them. They encountered the fury of the deep, riding fierce waves until their courage failed. They were at wit's end. But it only took a hand reached toward God. The storm hushed, and in His love, He guided them to harbor. Theirs was a horror story turned holy, and the Psalmist believed everyone should hear it (vv 23-32).

The entire end of Psalm 107 is about how God turned rivers into deserts when His people rebelled, and then turned deserts into rivers when they repented (vv 33-43). It paints a picture of their homecoming to a verdant land of flowing springs where they could settle down and make a life. God shifted the atmosphere and changed the outcome.

HE TURNED IT!

Then, He prospered their ways by making them fruitful and bountiful. Needy people found provision. Families flourished. The way God reversed their curse caused them to, *"Ponder the loving deeds of the Lord"* (v43b).

God is the master at flipping the script

When you tell your story as a *"redeemed"* person, you enhance the reputation and image of God. Your rescue, your restoration, is simply the account of how God flipped the script and rewrote the ending. What happened in your past only provides context for what God wants to do in your future.

Walk in the wonder of your own rescue, and you create opportunity for those who hear the story to wonder, "Who does that?" The story of how God turned it is an invitation to wonder.

Paul gives a beautiful description of what grace and redemption do in our stories. *"We have become his poetry, a re-created people that will fulfill the destiny he has given each of us, for we are joined to Jesus, the Anointed One. Even before we were born, God planned in advance our destiny and the good works we would do to fulfill it!"*[2]

God rewriting your story makes it beautiful—wonder-full, in fact. But that does not make it easy. There is no guarantee the plot will be safe or the story will make sense while it's unfolding.

But one thing is certain—if God writes the narrative, the ending will be epic.

Isaiah painted a profound picture of how this history-revising God does it. Jesus then adopted the Prophet's words as the plotline for His own story.

> *"The Spirit of the Sovereign Lord is on me, because the Lord has anointed me to proclaim good news to the poor. He has sent me to bind up the brokenhearted, to proclaim freedom for the captives and release from darkness for the prisoners, to proclaim the year of the Lord's favor and the day of vengeance of our God, to comfort all who mourn, and provide for those who grieve in Zion."*[3]

The Seer predicts and the Nazarene incarnates an intimate entrance into the real stories of real people who are experiencing real pain in their lives. Jesus' specific assignment and unique capacity was to step into dark places within the flow of human lives and shift the trajectory, so they finish at a better place. His chosen audience was the broken, the captive, the lost and the grieved. His goal was to scribe a better ending.

The outcome of this prophetic ministry in which Jesus trafficked was that He, *"bestows on them a crown of beauty instead of ashes, the oil of joy instead of mourning, and a garment of praise instead of a spirit of despair."*[4] Jesus delights in turning stories from ashes to beauty, from mourning to joy, from despair to praise.

No wonder David looked at his own checkered life and found reason for wonder. Only a good God can take such a terrible life and turn it into an epic biography. One day, when in His eternal presence we get to read the story of our lives from back to front, we'll stand in absolute awe and wonder of what He has done.

Why not start now? We should be dumbstruck at a God who so thoroughly rewrites our history that it leads to His destiny.

Breathtaking and beautiful, nothing in our stories ever goes to waste under the pen of the Author of life. It is fascinating to read the artistry of His imagination between the lines of our existence. Such creativity should leave us shaking our heads in wonder.

It's true, the story He writes hurts sometimes. There is no immunity from pain or brokenness in this world. But Jesus never wants us to go with the flow of those rivers of tears. His desire is to dam the flood and redirect the course so that you can rejoice in what you *go through* because of where you *go to*.

How you went through what you went through may well determine how you end up where you end up!

What you've experienced is necessary preparation for where He's leading you, what He's making you and how He's using you. The battles you've won prepare you for the war you'll fight. Past pain is the seedbed for future harvest.

> ## *Destiny is most often hidden in history*

Look at what comes from those lives once characterized by ashes and sorrow. *"They will be called oaks of righteousness, a planting of the Lord for the display of his splendor. They will rebuild the ancient ruins and restore the places long*

28

devastated; they will renew the ruined cities that have been devastated for generations. "[5] The very ones whose stories were tragedies found endings that were "happily ever after."

Not only did they get the *"instead"* replacements of beauty, joy and praise, those same broken-healed souls change the ending for so many other stories. These rescued and restored souls become sturdy oak trees that rebuild ruins, restore devastated places and rescue generations. When God rewrites the end of your story, He redrafts the narratives of those you influence. Our tales are never written in isolation.

David did not know that as a shepherd fighting ferocious animals God was equipping him to conquer fierce giants. He couldn't see that the giant who would stand before him required a lion and bear that lay behind him.

Dark chapters and dead ends do not diminish the wonder of any biography. We don't need to airbrush our portraits or sanitize our stories. Our histories do not require editing if we allow the Author to write *His*-story.

Your past doesn't define you. It prepares you.

PLOT TWISTS

"Each of us is a story, waiting for a devoted reader who will take us off the shelf and embrace all our plot twists."
~ John Mark Green

God has an uncanny ability to rewrite history as He authors destiny.

With Him, no matter where you are in the narrative, there's always more to the story. The chapter you're in is never the end. If you judge the book of your life by any single chapter or collected segment of them, you will always get the story wrong.

In the Spring of 2015, I became intimately acquainted with grief. Within three months, we faced the death of three family members.

My 36-year-old firefighter nephew just didn't wake up on a late March morning. I had no clue the day I performed his funeral that two weeks to the day later, I would bury my father. Just weeks after that funeral, my sweet mother-in-law, who had been in our home for over 15 years, passed away near age 98.

> "You discern my going out and my lying down. You are familiar with all my ways."
> ~Psalm 139:3

To say loss tried to come home to roost would be a massive understatement. Unexpected tragedy has a way of knocking us off the rails. It can send some people careening helplessly into chasms of grief and sorrow.

Those seasons of life can cause us to believe the plot of our lives has come unraveled. As if the Author had somehow lost track of the narrative flow. Suffering has an incredible ability to push a false narrative into the storyline of what had previously seemed a pleasant theme.

But pain doesn't present a problem to God. He can write into the plot of your story anything life throws at you. In the end, He always makes a better ending. The core of wonder is the way he weaves our worst into His best and creates texture, color and beauty out of what seemed like unusable stuff. He dips His quill in the inkwell of our experience and scribes a unique story that causes Heaven to dance and Hell to quake.

In their book, *You Can Trust God to Write Your Story,* Robert and Nancy Wolgemuth note, "Situations that seem confusing and chaotic to us are actually plot threads God is weaving together to create a story…a beautiful, compelling work of art."[1]

I vividly remember the time in my life when I believed I had a better grasp than God on how my story should go. I reached out in complete selfishness and dumped His inkwell. Inky darkness flooded over the book of my life. The storyline seemed completely lost. To anyone reading my life, it seemed there was nowhere to go with the narrative. Perhaps there was nothing more to my story.

But God dragged his pen through the puddle of black, turned the stained page, and with that very ink I spilled, started writing a new ending.

> ## The Author of Life is never stumped rewriting our history

When it seems we've ruined the story, Jesus will still write an alternative ending through the mess we've made. He has an ability to write every moment—no matter how dark or painful—into the plot and make the story richer, deeper and fuller. It doesn't even matter if the spilled the ink is our own fault. When Jesus recasts that mess, He makes history!

Wonder is most often written with dark ink.

Most of my reading these days is on my tablet, but there was a time when I had over 1500 print and ink books in my library. If you leafed through any of them, you'd find dog-eared pages with lots of yellow highlights. It would not be difficult for you to identify my favorite pages or words.

It occurred to me that some pages I'd like to rip out of the book of my life have become the dog-eared, highlighted parts of the story because they most shaped the plot. Many of the unwelcomed characters who've entered my narrative might well be the most valuable contributors to the flow of the Tale of Michael.

Paul Tripp insightfully said, "Thankfully, I am not the author of my own personal story. Your story isn't an autobiography either. Your story is a biography of wisdom and grace written by Another. Every turn He writes into your story is right. Every twist of the plot is for the best. Every new character or unexpected event is a tool of his grace. Each new chapter advances his purpose."[2]

That's why it so crucial to avoid getting stuck in any season. You just can't let any chapter define your entire story. No single season ever tells the whole truth. While none of us wants to endure dark seasons of failure, loss, pain or grief, God will turn the hard patches into rich nuance that makes the rest of the story the best of the story.

As long as He's still writing, there is always more to the story. God has a variety of climactic endings that He can attach to your story. He doesn't run out of plans for you. He is never at a loss for words.

Paul said it in now-famous words. *"We can be so sure that every detail in our lives of love for God is worked into something good."*[3] Jesus never loses track of the aim of the story—that we will come out looking like Him. God has factored into the flow of the biography all my frailties, faults and failures, and gets me where He wants me anyhow.

Don't scribble "The End" on a story
God is still writing!

Only when the Author of life lays the pen of time on the table of eternity is your story finished. His eulogy over your life is the only one that ultimately counts. He who is the *Author* is also the *finisher*.[4]

That word *"finisher"* means one who perfects or completes. God doesn't leave stories half-written. He never quits until the story reads just like He dreamed. His ending will be a masterpiece that will amaze us and make Him famous.

A tale of wonder.

Divine surprises are around every corner when we allow God to write as He deems best. He never ceases to amaze at the depth of His foresight and breadth of His insight. When the story is at an apparent dead end, God opens a hidden door so the adventure can continue. Like Narnia's wardrobe entrance, God's masterful ability to sneak the Kingdom in where you least expect it blows us away and bushwhacks our enemies.

David was all-to-familiar with derailing his life by choices he would later regret. Too frequently, He made a mess of the page God was writing. Some of those seasons seemed irredeemable. Some of those failures, irreparable. Some of his losses, unrecoverable.

Yet somehow David hung onto the better narrative—the one God was writing despite his own interruptions. He realized the story was bigger than him. In fact, all the pain and difficulty of real life gave color to the wonder God was creating.

Let his epic words soak in as you read them. *"God made my life complete when I placed all the pieces before him. When I got my act together, he gave me a fresh start. Now I'm alert to God's ways; I don't take God for granted. Every day I review the ways he works; I try not to miss a trick. I feel put back together, and I'm watching my step.* **God rewrote the text of my life when I opened the book of my heart to his eyes.** *"*[5]

God is skilled and proficient at plot twists. He will deposit something into the flow of your life-narrative that shifts the trajectory you hate and puts you on a path you will love. There's always the opportunity for an alternate ending. Your Author can flip the script. Trust His penmanship.

The End is never written in stone. Jesus rolled that away.

THE UNTOLD STORY

*"A story must be told or there'll be no story,
yet it is the untold stories that are most moving."*
~ J. R. R. Tokien

The wonderful American poet Maya Angelou once said, "There is no greater agony than bearing an untold story inside you." To have a tale to tell but feel your life is mute can demoralize. We each inherently know we are made for more—that we have an untold story that needs to be told. When the life we live and the story we carry don't align, the incongruity will paralyze passion.

I believe the most difficult part of faith isn't finding God in the trauma and tragedies of life. I have had substantial failure and suffered intense loss but have nearly always been able to see and feel Him close in those shadows.

In crisis seasons of my life—when failure disarmed me, frustration disillusioned me or fear disaffected me—Jesus was close and easy to embrace. Pain, sickness, poverty and loss have been most often accompanied by a visceral sense of His presence and compassion for me.

> *"Before a word is on my tongue you, Lord, know it completely."*
> *~Psalm 139:4*

Scripture says, *"God is close to the brokenhearted."*[1] He is really close when we really hurt.

For me, the toughest part of faith is digging Him out of the daily. Finding God in the rub and reality of mundane moments that are most of life is the greatest challenge to a life of wonder.

It's in the normal stuff of life, like the numbing rhythms of work, rest and play; the routines of making a living, paying the bills and life in a family—these common moments of *everydayness* are hard places to grab hold of Kingdom reality. They just seem too small to be "spiritual," too common to be "Kingdom."

> ## *It seems easier to find God in the dark than in the daylight*

He seems to show up for the big stuff, but I lose sight of Him when I'm sweating small stuff.

Jesus' preferred method of sketching *"on earth as in Heaven"* always involved stories. Each of His parables was dug directly out of the routines of life in His day. Look at the images He invokes in His stories.[2]

- Farm life (weeds, seeds and sheep)
- Household routines (lost coin, lighting lamps, sewing patches, making bread)
- Family realities (a prodigal son, a wedding and marriage feast, a pesky neighbor who wants bread at midnight)
- Relational conflict (specks and logs, forgiving debts quickly, helping neighbors in pain)
- Work stuff (fishing, investing and a rich fool)

The clearer Jesus wanted to be about Kingdom life in time and space, the more domestic and parochial the stories became.

My favorite of these tales is the parable of the treasure hunt. This story is a promise and a challenge. Look closely and you'll find Kingdom riches in the dirtiest, darkest and most desperate places.

"The kingdom of heaven is like treasure hidden in a field. When a man found it, he hid it again, and then in his joy went and sold all he had and bought that field."[3] It took only one verse for Jesus to show us how to hear the untold story of our lives.

The imagery is striking. A man is strolling through a field when, in a stroke of luck, he uncovers a hidden treasure. Its value was obvious, even if its location wasn't. Instead of stealing it and thus taking the chance of having to give it back, the man sells all he owns and buys the field so he can own the treasure.

Jesus made it clear through this parable that God hides His treasures in the "dirt" of our lives. To get the treasure, we must buy the field—a field worth more than all we have because of hidden treasure. Life for us as followers of Jesus is a constant treasure hunt where we are always on watch for divine surprises.

Herein is the lifestyle of wonder.

Solomon once said, *"It is the glory of God to conceal a matter; to search out a matter is the glory of kings."*[4] I think it goes something like this: God disguises who He is in the stuff of life as it is; we discover who we really are when we find Him there.

"Glory" appears twice in this maxim—once about God, once about kings. Glory has to do with the ultimate essence of something or someone. The glory of God is the truest part of who He is. The glory of man is the truest part of who we are.

Solomon points out that God's nature is to hide His true self in the messy business of the everyday. Not hiding from us, but for us. He tucks himself in a truth and buries that in your current situation. Then you uncover who you really are as you carefully investigate what God is hiding in your mess.

What glory hides in your mess?

The question is, what part of the Father's heart that you desperately need is hiding in your desperate circumstance? You will discover who you truly are as you explore who He is in your current situation.

That was Jesus' point as He constantly harped on one theme…the Kingdom of Heaven being *"at hand."* If it's at hand, it's close enough to touch. Yes, even right where you are. Everywhere, all the time, we are never far from the Kingdom.

That alone should lead to wonder.

Perhaps because of our thrill-seeking modern society or our big-event church culture, we are prone to look for God in big, bold, powerful places. You know, the "extraordinary" scenes like big revivals, dramatic encounters, crowded venues. Now there is no doubt He shows up in the wildest of places and the most unimaginable ways. But those are rare hiding places.

> *Life is a game of hide and seek for the eternal in the here and now*

We search out the Kingdom among diapers and dustpans; oil changes and car washes; making a living and paying the bills.

Unless and until I find Christ and His Kingdom in the ruts and routines of my ordinary life, the exceptional moments of divine breakthrough may actually be a distraction. An escape rather than engagement.

Perhaps we need to go back to a scene we mentioned earlier. Jesus grabbed a little kid, stood him or her in front of his Kingdom hotshots and said, *"Unless you become like this little child, you can't even see the Kingdom."*[5] That doesn't mean it isn't there, it simply means we cannot see what should be obvious to Kingdom people!

Jesus taught us to pray that our address would look like His address. His Kingdom and will *"on earth as in heaven."*[6] Well, at my address there is grass to mow, bushes to trim, laundry to do, bills to pay, cars to fix, family members to avoid killing…you get it?

If I am honest, my earth isn't very heavenly. My normal isn't very supernatural. My daily doesn't seem to have so much eternal quality. Yet Jesus said my prayer should be just that—Heaven should live in my house.

That is a radical idea.

We are to pray that in our sphere of influence, in our realm of existence, people would know God as He truly is. We desire His purpose to be gladly and perfectly accomplished. Not in the future, but now—just like it is in Heaven.

Jesus said that from the moment He was born in Bethlehem and walked dusty Galilean roads, *"the Kingdom of Heaven"*[7] has been here. So, the Disciple's Prayer isn't for the Kingdom to come as if it isn't currently present. It has been and is "at hand" for over two millennia. Instead, the prayer is that I *find* the Kingdom that already exists right where I am at any moment.

Here is the part that boggles the mind and incites breathless wonder.

Jesus said the Kingdom was present in Him. Then He promised that when God glorified Him through the Resurrection, He would send His Spirit to be with and in us. The presence of the Kingdom, *localized* in the person of Jesus, was *globalized* when His Spirit fell on and filled every believer.

> *My little world should look just like*
> *His big one*

The Kingdom is more *at hand* now than it was when Jesus walked the earth because it has lost physical and geographical limitations. Jesus wasn't kidding when He said, *"Greater works shall you do."*[8] The Kingdom is all around and within me, hidden in the ordinary realities of mundane and routine life.

It is my glory to find His glory there!

Children seem to have an incredible capacity to see this supernatural Kingdom hidden in the natural. It is easier for them than for "grown-ups." We get old and lose "holy imagination."

Sometimes through disappointment, often in disillusionment. It may lead us to waste our "expectant faith" on counterfeit escapism. Geriatric faith has a really hard time seeing the extra- in the ordinary.

That was the point of all Jesus' stories. The *hidden presentness* and the *present hiddenness* of the Kingdom.

That is the untold story.

HEADLINES &
DETAILS

"It's always good news when you're closer to the truth."
~ Fabiola Gianotti

The Sunday paper was once an afternoon pastime for most folks. No different for my wife, Dianne, and me. After morning church and Sunday lunch, we'd stop by the grocer, pick up the giant gazette and settle in for a few hours of flipping through its pages. Of course, with a gridiron backdrop on telly.

Truthfully, for Dianne it was hours. For me, minutes. As with most ladies, she read it all—from cover to cover. Me? Just headlines.

She'd laugh and ask, "You done already?" But really, how long can it take to read the front page, a magazine insert and the comics?

I know I've dated myself with that description since newspapers are nearly a thing of the past, but it illustrates a point. Some people are headline people. Others demand details.

God is not a headline person. He is way into details.

"You hem me in behind and before, and you lay your hand upon me."

~Psalm 139:5

David understood this so well. Brian Simmons beautifully captured the Psalmist's description of how God wrote the details of his life. *"You know every step I will take before my journey even begins. You've*

41

gone into my future to prepare the way, and in kindness, you follow behind me to spare me from the harm of my past."[1]

"Every step before I take it." That phrase literally means "you scattered my path before me." Talk about details! David declares before we ever took our first faltering step. God knew every footfall to the day we lay in a grave. In fact, He's gone into that future—seen the end from the beginning—to make sure our path aligns to His purpose.

God is literally obsessed with shaping your life into what He dreamed before you were born. He dreamed you up in His heart before He ever cooked you up in your mother's womb. He has an overarching desire that you meet His design.

God is deeply interested in the details of your destiny.

Us? We're far more concerned with destination. The trip isn't the thing, it's about where we wind up. We want to get where we're going as quickly as possible. God is much more concerned with who we end up being than where we end up going.

Destination is where you're going
Destiny is what you become on the way

I've written that phrase somewhere in each of my books and say it in nearly every sermon. It is a reminder I constantly need. Doubt I've ever understood anything so important. I am always trying to make it somewhere, while God is always trying to make me someone.

This single idea defines the difference between that little boy on the plane and the too-frequent flyers so numb to flying that we didn't experience the miracle of flight anymore. Every detail of the journey enamored—mesmerized, really—my little friend.

Wonder drains from our lives when we forget to remain present to the journey. An obsession with *arriving* short-circuits the journey of *becoming* every time.

The headline in your "now" might be adversity or struggle. But the details uncover meaning behind the mess, significance under the suffering, and purpose in the pain. God makes sure that all we endure fits into the bigger narrative He is unveiling.

Wonder always wonders, "What is the underlying storyline at the moment?"

To maintain a living sense of awe, we must go far deeper than headlines and pay attention to the details. Soundbites do not keep us afloat when we encounter mysteries that baffle us.

Peter described believers as *"exiles"* who live on foreign soil as aliens. His instruction for living in that uncharted territory? *"Live each day with holy awe and reverence throughout your time on earth."*[2] Despite the discomfort of being a stranger in a temporary home, we are to live amazed at Jesus, who fits us for our eternal home.

That is everyday wonder.

Considering the headlines of our day, this might seem like an exercise in futility. Carrying wonder in a world weighed down by confusion and catastrophe appears a bit too Ostrich-like for most. But it is not burying your head in delusional sand to believe there is Someone who will make sense of chaos. It's called hope—the rocket fuel of wonder.

If you really think about it, God has been doing this make-sense-of-chaos thing since before the beginning of time. God didn't sketch the beauty of order on a blank backdrop. He painted it on a canvas of grotesque disorder. Just as the Spirit brooded over the dark void *"in the beginning"*[3] and brought creation from chaos so He has the unique ability to change your trajectory mid-flight.

From the birth of time, God wanted us to know first and foremost, He is a god who cleans up hopeless situations! He wrote into creation's DNA that this was a God who made miracles from messes—creating all that exists from a primordial soup that was *"formless and empty."*

Chaos is Holy Spirit's home turf

It's where He does His best work! Within every incomprehensible, intolerable thing that happens in our lives, there is always the promise of new creation. The boiling cesspool of unrest, fear, dissension, sickness, grief and fragmentation is where He has home field advantage. We'll unpack this more shortly.

Wonder is not an oversimplification of the complexities of life as we know it. It is not reduction, but concentration. Not blurry-eyed optimism, but focused reality. Not watered-down life, but distilled living. In every mess life cooks up, there is inherent potential for the breathtaking creation of something so amazing it completes us and glorifies Him. This is how we walk in the atmosphere of awe.

Wonder can reemerge in us, even in the middle of massive trauma or unfathomable pain. Awake to the surprise presence of God in the dark corners of suffering, we experience a revival of wonder. Sacred imagination moves from speculation to participation. Divine dreams morph from ethereal to earthy.

To experience a life of awe, we must welcome the God who gets His hands dirty. There is such joy in knowing He's never afraid of the mess we're in. Remember, ours is a God who showed up in a stable and slept in a manger so we could know for certain there was nowhere He wouldn't go.

Because He came, there is always more to the story than the headlines.

The enemy of your soul is a master of writing shallow captions over your pain to create commotion and conduct fear. He determines to disorient you by serving you only bad news in its grossest form. Bent in duplicity and biased by deception, the narrative he offers comes in terse headlines with no eternal connection or spiritual context.

But God wants you to read the rest of the story. That's where the wonder is. In the details, we see God's hand as He turns the worst news into the best story.

The whole of Scripture is an aggregate of stories that should leave us speechless and scratching our heads. Real people with real names like Abraham, Jacob, Joseph, Esther, David, Ruth, Hosea—each saw God write the best stories under the worst headlines.

If we stop focusing on the headlines, we'll find Him in the details.

MYSTERY
WRITER

"The world, even the smallest parts of it,
is filled with things you don't know."
~ Sherman Alexie

In my neck of the woods, the Space Coast of central Florida, we still speak his name with a gentle sense of reverence. Neil Armstrong put our region on the map when he put his boots on the moon. Even though he walked on the moon, he never walked away from wonder. The main reason? He never got to the end of his list of questions. This moonwalker once said, "Mystery creates wonder and wonder is the basis of man's desire to understand." [1]

Our approach to mystery will determine whether we embrace or suffocate wonder. Mystery—the gift of not knowing it all—can either move us to marvel or drive us to madness.

> "Such knowledge is too wonderful for me, too lofty for me to attain."
> ~Psalm 139:6

Discomfort with our limited scope of understanding has driven many to create a manageable God. One they can explain, who always acts in ways that fit expectations. But what good is a manageable God when my life becomes unmanageable? How does a God who makes sense help me when my life doesn't?

Being at peace with mystery, the sections and seasons of my life I just can't explain, is critical to maintaining and expanding a sense of wonder.

I truly need a God who is constantly leaving me with more questions than answers.

If I can figure Him out, he isn't big enough!

As Psalm 139 continues its deep dive into the wonder of human living, the poet admits the whole thing overwhelms him. *"Too wonderful"* to take in (v 4). If something is too wonderful, it magnifies wonder precisely because that thing is beyond comprehension. It's too high for me to grasp, way over my head. This mystery I face, this understanding I seek, is far above my pay grade.

But it's all part of God's plan. Mystery is God playing hide and seek with His kids. Jesus said the Father purposely hid the mystery so we would have to be curious kids to unearth it.

God is the ultimate Mystery Writer

Listen to Jesus' declaration about the Kingdom. *"I thank you, Father, Lord of heaven and earth, that you have **hidden** these things from the wise and understanding and **revealed** them to little children; yes, Father, for **such was your gracious will.**"*[2]

The word *"hidden"* in Greek is *krypto*. I bet you heard the word we derive from it—*encryption*. God encrypted the mysteries of the Kingdom in your down-to-earth ordinary life. What to my "adult" minds often feels like a morass of unanswered question, to the childlike heart of a Jesus-follower is a treasure chest of what I can discover.

In the treasure field story I mentioned earlier, what the man found was *"hidden"* in the field.[3] Only because he was paying attention on his journey did he unearth this prize that changed his entire life.

Oddly enough, this stash was hiding in plain sight. There is no sign this fellow was on a planned treasure hunt. He was simply walking with eyes wide open. Many others had likely passed the same way, but indifference caused distraction and they inadvertently missed something of high worth.

The treasure in Jesus' story is that hidden but at-hand Kingdom. Someone concealed it purposefully in a place that would escape casual notice. Premeditatedly placed where you would least expect it. The Greek word includes the idea of a valuable set in a secret place with the expectation anyone really looking would find it.

Buried in plain sight.

Much of Kingdom reality starts with seeing what no one else does in a situation. Finding God where others think He might not be. Reading between the lines in life.

> Kingdom eyes see what is hiding
> in plain sight

Jesus' brief story of the treasure in the field unlocks this phenomenon. There are a few things that have emerged for me from this single verse about Kingdom stuff hidden in plain sight. Mystery just beneath the surface.

What's Hidden In Mystery Is Bigger Than We Imagine

Jesus identifies the treasure as *"the Kingdom of Heaven."* Heaven is the place that unquestioningly welcomes God's reign. His will done joyfully. His sovereignty unimpeded, unquestioned, unrivaled. The Kingdom on earth is where that same atmosphere exists now, here, among us. Seeking and finding this Kingdom is the single trait that makes life an adventure instead of a burden.

What's Hidden In Mystery Has Incredible Value

The word *"Treasure"* means both deposit and depositary. The treasure and the vessel in which you place a valuable for safekeeping. When the King of everything says we should value a thing as *"treasure,"* we dare not question its worth. Yet the problem with finding treasure in our mundane living is we underestimate the worth of small things. Culture constantly defines "valuable" as what is in, trending or hot. What society esteems as treasure makes us lose sight of the value of the commonplace—that which actually is uncommonly good.

We need to stop finding relevance in a scene that is irrelevant to the Kingdom. Valuing what is valuable maintains the hot edge of wonder.

What's Hidden In Mystery Is Secret For A Reason

Hiding implies the one who hid the treasure wanted it discovered. But only by someone who understood its value, no matter where he found it. Someone who noticed because he was aware and alert. Not a passer-by, but a seeker. Even when Jesus came and tented among people, we missed Him. And He was the very expression of the Kingdom among us. If the world didn't notice God himself hiding among them, how easy to miss His Kingdom if we're not looking.

What's Hidden In Mystery Is Closer Than We Think

The *"field"* was a place where men worked, produced crops and reaped a harvest. In the field, human effort met created purpose and produced profit. It didn't matter if the lucky treasure finder was working, walking or wandering. He was near a Kingdom that was present whether or not he saw it! The eternal in the earthy is sometimes too close to see when we think that nothing good could be there.

What's Hidden In Mystery Is Seen Only By Seekers

Finding comes only after seeking. The traveler uncovered the treasure because he was paying attention with intention. The treasure was hidden on purpose so only those who correctly valued it can find it. Only those who are compelled with passion and desire grab what is at hand. You will never do greater things if you are distracted by lesser things. Even more, you never see greater things if you don't first see greatness in lesser things.

What's Hidden In Mystery Changes The Finder

When the seeker finds the treasure, he alters his valuation of the field. He assesses the field differently. Knowing the buried treasure was there caused the field itself to become a treasure. The seeker who is now the finder re-hides the treasure because he now knew this field had intrinsic value. So he bought it. With *"joy"* he sold all and bought the field.

When we find Kingdom value in our everyday existence, we attribute new value to the everyday. Discovering God's gifts in daily of life creates joy, so the daily becomes our treasure hunt. We become wonder-walkers.

If Jesus was about anything, he was about turning the ordinary into extraordinary. He constantly filled the temporal with eternal value. Above everything, Jesus was above "sacramental."

Sacrament is an external, visible sign of an internal, spiritual reality. Take the most mundane, normal things, fill them with rare, remarkable value and you have a sacrament. God does it all the time. He hides the most incredibly valuable things in the most inanely normal places.

It's a mystery how The King does it; how he hides such treasure in jars of clay. But as we explore—spelunking in the depths of the Spirit—we find wonder in the glory.

DISCOVERY

God Is Fully Present
At The End Of
All My "Ifs"

Psalm 139:7-12

Where can I go from your Spirit? Where can I flee from your presence? If I go up to the heavens, you are there; if I make my bed in the depths, you are there. If I rise on the wings of the dawn, if I settle on the far side of the sea, even there your hand will guide me, your right hand will hold me fast. If I say, "Surely the darkness will hide me and the light become night around me," even the darkness will not be dark to you; the night will shine like the day, for darkness is as light to you.

WHAT IF?

*"What if everything that happened here,
happened for a reason?"*
~ John Locke

Children don't think to ask the question. Perhaps that's why they try so many crazy things without giving the first thought to risk. In a kid's head adventure holds sway over sensibility. The potential fun far outweighs the practical fallout. Two little words might avoid some serious pain.

"What if?"

What if this homemade cape doesn't really help me fly when I jump off this roof? What if my tongue won't get unstuck from this frozen pole? What if my bike can't make it to the other side of that ditch? What if this permanent marker really is permanent? What if this text picture doesn't really disappear from cyberspace?

Frequently, children or teens end up in situations that leave their parents shaking their heads and bewilderedly asking, "Why would you do that?" Mainly, the kid just never really considered the outcome.

> *"Where can I go from your Spirit? Where can I flee from your presence?"*
> *~Psalm 139:7*

Flip the dare coin and you'll see adults probably ask that question too much. Since grownups feel they know the answer, they slap limits on the chances they take. So much so that the potential for joyous adventure seeps from life simply because we refuse to see anything chancy worth the gamble. There is an inherent fear in us that drives us to run from risk.

We see the opportunity to do something amazing, but when we weigh the risk, we turn tail and run.

But here's the hard truth: a life of wonder requires risk!

David lived on that risky edge often as He faced God's desires for him. The Divine challenges scared the bejabbers out of him. He often wanted to run for his life and put some distance between him and a God who wanted to stretch his limits.

I get it. Sometimes I just want to hightail it from the God who pursues me. What He dreams for me is so far beyond what I think I can do, that it feels safer to pull a Jonah and book it fast and far in the wrong direction.

The problem with risking it all is the potential for losing it all. But that is the inherent code of honor in the Kingdom of God. Risk and loss are the evidence of chasing a God who is always on the move in ways we seldom understand.

Following Jesus involves immersion in a Kingdom culture where the full scope of life bows to the active reign of God. Jesus said it was our aim to *"seek first the Kingdom of God and His righteousness."*[1]

Kingdom culture is earth looking a lot like Heaven.

> ## *Kingdom is when my address looks like His address*

To have this kind of Kingdom *"on earth as it is in heaven"* demands risk. We leave the "what ifs" to the only One who knows the answer. Feeling the loss is a prerequisite to finding the treasure.

As I write this, people all around me are tallying up the answers to some of the hardest "what ifs" I've seen in all my years. Mourning and grief are universal experiences of the pain of genuine loss.

These words feel somewhat capricious and shallow since corporately we have just lived through a season of indescribable loss.

- Lost loved ones
- Lost relationships
- Lost health
- Lost alliances
- Lost hope

None of us want to, but all of us will walk through that valley of the shadow of death at some point. Seems recently many have.

Yet Paul says to the church at Thessalonica: *"We do not want you to be uninformed, brothers, about those who are asleep, that you may not grieve as others do who have no hope."*[2]

That one word—*hope*—transforms "what if" from a question of fear to one of faith. Hope is jet fuel for a life of wonder. Facing the future with hope, we are free to walk through the present in wonder. The uncertainty of "what if" realities dissipates as we revel in mystery and the freedom of not knowing it all.

> *Hope changes grief from a dead-end*
> *to a pathway through the pain*

David paints the picture beautifully when he describes the journey of those who follow God's heart.

> *"Blessed are those whose strength is in you,*
>   *whose hearts are set on pilgrimage.*
> *As they pass through the Valley of Baka (tears),*
>   *they make it a place of springs;*
>   *the autumn rains also cover it with pools.*
> *They go from strength to strength,*
>   *till each appears before God in Zion."*[3]

Jesus says much the same thing when in His second beatitude He triumphantly declares, *"Blessed are those who mourn for they will be comforted."*[4] An incredulous oxymoron. Two disparate ideas held in a taut but harmonic tension.

This is hope for the risk-taker who wants to answer the "what if" ambiguity of life with the "what's more" wonder of the Kingdom.

With this crazy Kingdom Blessing, Jesus lays before us three distinct realities of life in this world.

Within the challenge is a promise: **You Can Flourish In A World of Loss.**

"Blessed." Such a word of hope. It is so much more than happy. Blessed means supremely fortunate. In this state, we live independent of surroundings. Here is a place of deep trust and satisfaction in reality as God defines it.

Simultaneously, Jesus recognizes pain: **You May Hurt In A World of Loss.**

Our Savior never relied on some panacea to create a sense of hope for His followers. If Jesus was anything, He was raw and real—hardcore honest about life on a broken planet.

"Mourn" carries a sense of deeply feeling grief over the loss of a person or thing that was valued and loved. It is the strongest word for mourning or grieving available to Jesus. It describes being dazed and confused by what you've been through.

Mourning is essentially homesickness. In grief, we get lost in our own story. We know things are not as they are supposed to be. Something is missing. More accurately, Someone is missing.

The blessing of loss comes when risk pursued creates a vulnerability that invites Presence. **You Will Find God In A World of Loss.**

Those who mourn in the Kingdom will be *"comforted."* In its original form, this is a fascinating word. Almost identical to the name Jesus gave to Holy Spirit, the ever-present Companion who was coming.

The Comforter. Mourning in Kingdom Culture invites the *presence* of a person—the Comforter—not merely the *presents* of soothing words. Comfort lies in the presence that heals by proximity.

Eugene Peterson captures it in his paraphrase. *"You're blessed when you feel you've lost what is most dear to you. Only then can you be embraced by the One most dear to you."*[5]

At the end of "what if" stands a Person whose very presence causes all you've been through make eternal sense. That is the ultimate wonder.

IF ONLY

"If only…
the saddest words in the English language."
~ Kristan Higgins

Some of my favorite childhood memories have to do with holidays. Especially as it relates to food. My mother could cook with the best of them, and our family celebrations were absolute feasts. On holidays, friends and relatives crammed around sumptuous tables filled with all the delicacies we craved during the rest of the year's ordinary days.

The only drawback? There was never enough room for everyone at the main table. That's why Mom created alternative seating for those who had a chronological deficit! Usually a card table, it was the place away from the grown-ups where we would devour dinner and eagerly long for dessert.

The "kid's table," she called it. As baby of a large family, I spent most of my life there.

Through my childhood I sat at that table musing melancholically, "If only I was old enough to eat at the big table." As if there was something better about being with a bunch of old people. The day I graduated to the big table, I knew I'd arrived.

"If I go up to the heavens, you are there; if I make my bed in the depths, you are there."
~Psalm 139:8

I quickly realized the kid's table was a much better place to eat. The older I got, the more I thought "if only I was young enough to eat at the kid's table!"

This might be a dilemma that transcends family meals. We seem to always wish we were at a different table, with different people, enjoying different food.

Always troubled by two silly words that rob the present of its salient beauty. Two words that suck the oxygen of wonder from the room.

"If only."

I read David's famous Psalm 23 and thought about the kid's table. In the middle of the famous poem is an odd phrase, raising a strange mental picture when taken at face value.

"You prepare a table before me in the presence of my enemies."[1]

A battlefield seems a weird place to eat! But that's the picture. It's as if David is saying, "As you pursue God, the enemy throws trouble at you. The harder you chase God, the bigger the obstacles you'll encounter." But...

There's a table in your trouble!

This is no ordinary table, either. The Hebrew word *"table"* means "spread"—like a smorgasbord. This is a feast at a king's table. We might be in a war zone, but we're not stuck with MREs!!

And it's *"prepared"*—carefully, thoughtfully put in place. Ordered and ordained. Specific food for specific need. God has a feast in the oven before the enemy makes his first move. Checkmate before the match starts.

He sets this table *"before me."* Literally, before my face; before my eyes. It is personal. It's your trouble, so He sets your table! The table is both for "me" *and* "my enemies" to see the goodness and power of God in the middle of the battle.

He makes a point of it. The table is in the presence of *"enemies."* There's a lot of them and they are bent on ambush. The word for enemies means "to bind; constrict; lock up." These enemies want to choke the life and drain the wonder from you. But when the enemies hem you in and are sure they have you, God turns that place into a picnic!

As far as David is concerned, hell only observes what Heaven offers. *"In the presence"* means right in front of them. All up in the face of my enemies so they can't miss it. They thought they had you, but now they must watch you feast. God's table in my trouble is a declaration to my enemies that they have messed up!

Job, the Bible's oldest book, declares:

*But those who suffer he delivers **in** their suffering;*
  *he speaks to them **in** their affliction.*
"He is wooing you from the jaws of distress
  to a spacious place free from restriction,
  *to **the comfort of your table laden with choice food.**"*[2]

Jehovah God prepares this table. He sets it, serves it; and does the dishes! Why? To show the enemy who he's messing with. God stands at the end of our "if only" to remind both us and the enemy that in the end, God is in the end!

Another thought rose from David's intriguing picture. If God spreads this table on a battlefield, all the while I'm feasting, somebody else must be fighting. While I am sitting at the table God set for me, He is executing vengeance on my enemies. Simply breathtaking!

Most of the time we want hard times to end. Yet, there is a table available where we feast and God fights for us. "If only" is the short-sighted longing of a short-circuited heart. We dare not long for a change that could rob us of His blessing.

The feast feeds the fire of the future

David lived a scenario fully illustrating these lyrics of his song. We find it in the middle of his biography.[3] It's rooted in a deep relationship he shared with Saul's son, Jonathan. Theirs may have been the friendship Solomon later referenced when he mentioned *"a friend who is closer than a brother."*[4]

David wanted to restore dignity to Jonathan's name and line. He investigated whether there were any descendants of his friend to whom he could show favor. That's when he unearthed the painful story of Mephibosheth.

Jonathan chose a name with dream and destiny attached. The funny sounding name means, "to dispel shame by crushing it to pieces; to exterminate idols." This boy's destiny was to crush anything that raised itself in competition with God. He was designed to crush idols.

But something happened.

As Saul's kingdom was crumbling, his family and colleagues in the palace ran for their lives. A horrible accident happened on the way out. The nanny for five-year-old Mephisbosheth dropped him and he came up lame. Maimed and disabled for life. Idol slayer no longer. His identity as heir to the throne and nemesis to idolatry lost to his lameness. Simply because somebody dropped him.

Saul's family hid the broken boy. Separated and marginalized, he was to end his life alone. Impertinent, abandoned and unnoticed.

Until one day a king came along who saw him differently. David understood his worth because he valued the lame man's heritage. *"Is there anyone from my best friend's house I could honor?"*

Sounds so much like the King of Kings, whose heart is always searching for someone to restore. *"For the eyes of the Lord run to and fro throughout the whole earth, to show Himself strong on behalf of those whose heart is loyal to Him."*[5]

When David heard the somber saga of his best friend's son, he had him *"...brought from Lo Debar."* The name fit the place well. Lo Debar "not a pasture; not a word." A depressing place where he lived in the House of Makir like a slave. But in this broken place, he captured the attention of a benevolent king.

> *There was no evil intention here*
> *This was not a king to fear*

Mephisbosheth may well have thought David was going to exact revenge. That's the way most kings treated the family members of their predecessors. But David was a different kind of king. When the young man was brought before him, David called him by the name Jonathan had given him. It was a gesture that restored dignity to his identity.

David allayed the man's terror with these words. *"I will surely show you kindness."* Here was a merciful king who trafficked in favor.

The promise was breathtaking to the man defined by his limitation. *"I will restore your fortunes."* David gave him back what he had lost because life had broken him. The King restored everything lost by accident, anything purposely stolen, all that was rightfully his because it belonged to the family inheritance.

All of it restored by a King who didn't label him lame

Then comes the most amazing offer of all. *"You will always eat at my table."* *Table*—there's that same word used by this same David in Psalm 23. "From this point on, you will feast at my spread."

Yet, for total restoration, something had to happen in Mephibosheth not just for him. Listen to the pain in his response. *"Why would you bless me, a dead dog?"* That term, "dead dog," was an idiom for the male prostitutes who served at pagan shrines. Can you see how deeply his identity was broken?

He was built to slay idols. Instead, he saw himself enslaved to them.

Even with all Mephibosheth lost restored, David understood Jonathan was gone and his lame son would never live like a king on his own. David made sure this broken man understood the profound change taking place. From this point forward, the Crown—not the crowd—would define Mephibosheth.

"You will eat at my table like one of the king's sons." The rejected kid with the bad legs was to have a permanent place at the king's table as a king's son.

Whenever Mephibosheth's lame legs slid up under the King's table, you couldn't tell the difference between the cripple and the King's kids. Lame legs no longer mattered. Nobody even noticed. This crippled man, trapped in the broken legacy of a decimated lineage, restored to the King's table. The one place he would never have imagined sitting again.

Every meal was a take-your-breath-away experience of wonder.

I'm sure he bemoaned, *"if only,"* ever since someone dropped him. But then he discovered there was a table in the trouble.

EVEN IF

"What's worth doing even if you fail?"
~ Brené Brown

Death has an uncanny ability to re-focus life.

Seasons of loss revalue, refocus, refine and reignite living if we will listen to the life-message death declares. As I write this chapter, we are near the end of a season characterized by death. People, dreams, routines, jobs—so much has died. Few things have been more viscerally and violently shaken during this time than "church."

What we've known corporately and communally as the normal expression of the Body of Jesus is now fundamentally redefined. In this shaking, some things become clear if we're willing to hear them.

- If a Covid pandemic has shown us anything, it is that Church *can be* different.
- If the New Testament tells us anything, it is that the Church *will be* different.
- If current culture demands anything, it is that the Church *must be* different.

"If I rise on the wings of the dawn,
if I settle on the far side of the sea, even there..."
~Psalm 139:9-10a

This season of death has demanded and defined *different*. Radical redefinition fell on the church without warning or precedent. It changed us.

This season forced us to find wonder in a wilderness.

But we can't afford to forget a central reality. Since His resurrection, death has a different message. Death now speaks life.

It is this prophetic, revelatory quality of death that screamed at me recently as I read a familiar passage from the Old Testament prophet Isaiah. His encounter with God served as a prototype of "presence transformation." It came on the heels of his greatest loss.

"In the year that King Uzziah died I saw the Lord..."[1]

Many people think this was the moment of Isaiah's call. I don't. The young prophet had already experienced a divine call. He'd been preaching and prophesying to the leaders and people of Israel for a while.

The first five chapters of his book record him receiving powerful visions of judgment, restoration—history before it was made; the future long before it became present. He had even prophesied Jesus as a *"righteous branch"* who would one day rise.[2] Isaiah was standing firmly in the stream of revelation when something happened to him that amped up that revelation to a completely different level.

This moment in Isaiah 6 isn't a call, it's a confrontation. Here was a challenge for Isaiah to radically alter his approach to life, his view of the world and his understanding of God. The death of a single man in a single moment shifted everything for him. God had the Prophet's full attention.

> *This wasn't about life as it was*
> *but life as it should be*

We need a bit of the backstory of King Uzziah.[3] He ascended to the throne at age 16. This teenaged monarch launched a massive cultural revival. He and Isaiah became comrades. Together, they strategized at the palace and worshipped at the Temple.

Uzziah (sometimes called Hezekiah) was a loyal seeker of God who lived a godly life. God's hand was on him, so the King prospered. A Renaissance man, he excelled in theology and agriculture. He also mastered the strategies of war and amassed an army of elite troops. He built great towers and fortified the capital, Jerusalem. He even created "engines" designed to automate warfare.

This King was beloved by his people and feared by his enemies. His fame reached as far as Egypt. But Matthew recorded his greatest accolade much later in his gospel, placing Uzziah's name in the genealogy of Jesus.

Sadly, Uzziah's end was not august. His attempt to function inappropriately as a priest left him leprous. But even an inauspicious end didn't lower the King's value to Isaiah, who wrote the official biography of Israel's longest reigning king who ushered in a golden age.

Now we have a better grip on why when Isaiah mentions Uzziah's death, he is unveiling a life-shaking, soul-shaping moment in his own life. Isaiah was saying, "In the year I lost the only King I ever trusted, I met the only King I ever needed." The loss of what mattered to Isaiah exposed what counted to God.

> ## In his greatest loss, he gained
> ## his greatest gift

The darkest moment of his life illuminated by the brightest light of eternity. An encounter with Presence where God confronted his man with a fundamental truth. If you want to know what's really happening around you, look up, not down.

When everything seems to fall apart, look to God in the mess. This was an *"even if"* moment in Isaiah's life. Even if the worst happened, Isaiah learned God is always present—perhaps even more present in such moments of loss.

Isaiah *"saw the Lord."* When he did, everything else looked different.

Seeing God shook everything in which he trusted. He'd been looking at life from earth into the Heaven and it was overwhelming. When he saw the Lord, he saw from Heaven to earth. Yes, it rattled his cage, but he grasped how God lives on the other side of loss.

I discovered something here. John references these very words of Isaiah and explains them like this. *"Isaiah said this because he saw Jesus' glory and spoke about him."*[4] The glory Isaiah saw was that of Jesus alive at the Father's right hand. Isaiah gained a new point of view because He saw a new side of God.

Sometimes God can only reveal more of Himself after shaking loose our previous understanding. Seeing Jesus as He is *NOW* changes how we are *NOW*.

It steels us to say, "even if" life falls out in ways I never expected, my Jesus still reigns.

Isaiah came out of this encounter with three unwavering convictions.

GOD HAS SOMETHING DEEP TO RESTORE IN US

The young prophet saw himself accurately when he saw God clearly. Seeing God left him broken—*"ruined"* he called it. The prophet lost his voice. Speechless because he saw what a mess he was compared to what a wonder God was.

He also had a very important revelation about the place where he lived. *"I live among a people"* who are unclean and misdirected. A chosen family with no sense of purpose, no grasp on identity.

Isaiah's vision revealed not only his need for restoration, but God's desire to heal him. Even if he was a complete failure in that moment, God committed to make him whole.

GOD HAS SOMETHING REAL TO RELEASE THROUGH US

Isaiah saw God's heart, and it was compelling. God has always desired to have partners who express him accurately in the context in which He placed them. Re-presenting Him to a world without a clue.

"Then I heard..." Isaiah couldn't hear correctly until he experienced the touch of God's grace. God's call was clear. *"Who will go for us?"* Who will go embody us? Who will live in a way that the people I love can see what I'm really like?

"Send me..." Seeing the Lord and hearing His heart transformed the young prophet. Isaiah now believed He could express the God he'd encountered.

Restored hearts see and hear differently

After the breaking, he possessed a holy passion undiluted by unholy ambition. He understood what mattered to the Father. He accepted the challenge of facing his world with the fiery passion they wanted to ignore.

God challenged him to prophesy in the face of a world that plugged its ears and shaded its eyes. Even if they were unwilling to see or hear, preach anyhow. Why?

Because God had something more important in mind than changing minds. He was about winning hearts.

GOD HAS SOMETHING BIG TO REVEAL TO US

God was telling the prophet, "Even if they don't listen, you keep telling them about me and showing them what I look like. Even if the whole of your life and ministry looks like a deforested field of stumps, you keep prophesying. Preach to the stumps, Isaiah!"

Stumps may scream death, finality, barrenness, but *"the substance of life is still in the stump."* God showed Isaiah the seed of hope in the stump of despair. There is holy seed in those stumps! Significant change comes from the smallest things in the worst circumstances.

If there is seed left in it, God can birth life through it.

Isaiah saw the tragedy of David's great royal dynasty cut down to a stump! Israel's kings would all fail. None would lead the nation into covenant faithfulness. But there was holy seed that would rise from that stump of Jesse!

Even if you come to the end of all you've known and all you can see is a field of stumps, remember there is seed in the stump! Death is never an end to One who freely dispenses resurrection life. From Heaven's perspective, there is always life left in what death took.

Grab onto the truth that God never runs out of ideas, options, plans or remedies. You'll be free to walk in wonder.

IF THEN

"We must be willing to let go of the life we have planned,
so as to have the life that is waiting for us."
~ E. M. Forster

It happened on Pentecost Sunday 2021, smack in the middle of the greatest upheaval I've seen in my 62 laps around the sun.

We were in the middle of a pandemic. Churches, businesses, events, stores—Covid had shut down much of the country. The death of George Floyd punctured a festering wound lying just beneath the surface of the country's harmonious facade.

Unemployment was sky high as the government tossed out money like candy at a parade. These government bailouts turned into political cannon fodder, disintegrating any sense of civility in our land. Divisive dissent and distrust shredded neighborhoods, civic clubs, churches and even families.

It was the most frightening, disorienting and heartbreaking season of my life. As I scanned the landscape of culture, I saw what is most accurately characterized by a single word: chaos.

> "Even there your hand will guide me, your right hand will hold me fast."
> ~Psalm 139:10

Sitting in church that Sunday morning as we focused on the outpouring of the Holy Spirit,[1] something quietly resonated inside me like a whisper in a hurricane. What I heard startled me.

"Chaos is Holy Spirit's home turf."

I sat stunned. Could that be true? Was that really God speaking to my heart? Because if it was true, God meant that at the place of deepest disturbance and most aggressive agitation, Holy Spirit was most at home. The boiling cesspool of unrest, fear, dissension, sickness, grief and fragmentation was His home field advantage.

Precisely there—in the middle of unexplainable and intractable disorder—the Holy Spirit, by His mere presence, shifts the atmosphere and changes the outcome.

Chaos is the place of His finest work

To grasp the essence of this whisper, I needed to understand what *"chaos"* really was. By every definition, it is complete disorder or utter confusion. But almost without fail, to explain the full implication of chaos, even atheists refer to "the formless matter that existed before the creation of the universe." It appears nothing can sum up the reality of chaos like the "stuff" from which God made the world.

Something important came into focus. To understand the chaos we are currently experiencing, we need to look back to the very start.

"In the beginning..."[2]

Before anything at all existed, there was God, in His perfection and fulness. He existed as complete, without need. But that doesn't really capture it. God didn't exist, He WAS existence. *"Before the mountains were born, or you brought forth the earth and the world, **from everlasting to everlasting you are God.**"*[3] In the beginning, God was everything there was.

At the other end of time, John the Revelator heard the same thing resonate in Heaven. *"Worthy are You, our Lord and our God, to receive glory and honor and power; for **You created all things**, and because of Your will they existed, and were created."*[4]

This God, who was all of existence—consummate and transcendent—had a driving passion to create this universe. The God who needed nothing, wanted something. This desire wasn't about stars or mountains or oceans or eagles or any of the stuff that amazes us. Isaiah spoke of God *"who created the heavens...who fashioned and made the earth, he founded it; he did not create it to be empty but **formed it to be inhabited.**"*[5]

Driven by this fervor for a people, God *"created the heavens and the earth."* Significantly, Scripture establishes a very important fact about this design He was making—*God created everything from nothing.*

The author of Hebrews says it this way, *"For every house is built by someone, but the builder of all things is God"* (Hebrews 3:4). He added, *"the universe was formed at God's command, so that what is seen was not made out of what was visible."*[6]

John wrote, *"All things were made through (Jesus), and without him was not anything made that was made."*[7] Paul concluded, *"...all things have been created through him and for him. He is before all things, and in him all things hold together."*[8] It appears this God-creating-from-nothing idea is pretty important.

Now, look again at Genesis 1. *"Now the earth was formless and empty, darkness was over the surface of the deep."*[9] The Message translation gives us a vivid picture: *"Earth was a soup of nothingness, a bottomless emptiness, an inky blackness."*

Here's the big question that haunted me that Pentecost Sunday. If God created from nothing—because nothing existed with Him in the beginning—then where did the formless/void/dark earth come from?

That chaos had to come from somewhere. God created from nothing, so chaos could not have existed when there was nothing but God in the beginning. If He created from nothing, as Scripture frequently confirms, then it appears He had to be the one who *created the chaos out of which Creation ultimately emerged.*

GOD WAS THE ONE BEHIND THE CHAOS!

If this were not true, the Genesis account would start something like this, *"In the beginning, God created the heavens and the earth...And God said, Let there be light..."* Instead, we have this inserted picture that before there was creation, there was chaos.

God made a mess before He made the world

Earth was a cosmic soup with no clearly discernible features. Essentially, a mass of raw materials. The magnificent beauty and complexity of the natural world and each of its human inhabitants rose from this orderless vacuum. God didn't sketch Creation on a blank backdrop. He painted it on a canvas of grotesque disorder.

Now I can smell the smoke rising from under many collars at this point. Doesn't fit neatly into our theological framework, this God as author of chaos thing. How can a good God create chaos? For Him to make chaos is just so out of character. After all, didn't Paul say, *"God is not the author of confusion but of peace."*[10]

But I would submit that God creating this primordial stew fits His character and nature perfectly. Because the "chaos" of time's beginning wasn't evil like some primordial demonic stew. It was just random disorder. Empty. Dark. Formless. Like a puzzle dumped out of a box, the pieces scattered carelessly on the tabletop. Yet, that cosmic cauldron of empty darkness was the womb of all that we now see and know.

God knew long before He spoke one star into space that man would sin and release chaotic ruin into His perfect creation. He also already knew He would come and fix the mess we made.

God made a mess that had a message

Paul speaks of the *"mystery that has been hidden and that God destined for our glory before time began."*[11] Before creation, Jesus sat with the Father in all His perfection and splendor.[12] But prior to creation, Jesus was also crucified, resurrected and exalted. He *"was chosen before the creation of the world,"*[13] and was *"the Lamb...slain from the creation of the world."*[14]

God dreamed of a Kingdom of redeemed people who would willingly partner with Him out of deep gratitude and love. From that dream, He created a realm Jesus referred to as *"the kingdom prepared for you* (mankind) *since the creation of the world."*[15]

Was there purpose in this pre-creation chaos? God appears to say, "what I want you to know about me first and above all is that I am a God who cleans up hopeless messes!"

How did all the beauty, wonder, complexity and grandeur of creation come to be? What turned the chaos into creation?

"Darkness was over the surface of the deep, and the Spirit of God was hovering." Like a mother hen incubating her eggs, Holy Spirit brooded over that primeval chaos. *"The Spirit of God brooded over the waters."* Darkness was over the deep. Holy Spirit was over the darkness.

Chaos is holy spirit's home turf!

Out of that unfathomable darkness came light, beauty, life and ultimately, us. Holy Spirit brooding over the waters changed something in that void. It made God's voice irresistible. All that was needed was a whisper to the chaos for creation to erupt.

Here's the point. God baked restoration into creation. It was already here when we arrived!

Oh friend, within every mess in life there is the potential for the breathtaking creation of something so amazing that it completes us and glorifies Him. No matter the chaos, He still creates.

Too often we think, *"If* _____ (insert your terrible fear) happens, *then* _____ (insert your feared result) will inevitably occur." But God is a master of reworking *then* no matter the *if*!

This is our hope for the seasons of sorrow or pain in this broken but beautiful world! Holy Spirit is brooding in every period of pain to nourish the hidden seed of hope and create life beyond the ifs. It may look like…

- Things are out of control.
- Darkness is winning.
- People have lost their minds.
- Principalities of Hell have taken the reins.
- Disease is on an unstoppable rampage.

But the Spirit is brooding. He is a master at using the chaos we face to create something so amazing we will thank God for what we went through because of how we came out! Remember, chaos is Holy Spirit's home field advantage. He specializes in making unbelievable miracles from unimaginable messes. He is a master at transforming dead-ends into open doors and blind alleys into portals of glory.

Now that I think about it, wonder as a perpetual response to this incomprehensible God is making a lot more sense.

AS IF

"Whenever you do a thing,
act as if all the world were watching."
~ *Thomas Jefferson*

Wonder is fascination that captivates the mind, heart and attention. It keeps us focused on God's face, attentive to His moving and responsive to His heartbeat. Without wonder, other loves easily capture our affection.

But life often throws shade at Wonder. As the hymn writer noted, sometimes "darkness veils His lovely face." We feel the absence of the ever-present one; the silence of Him whose words are "Spirit and life."

In his Psalm of wonder, David states that one extremity he tested, one of the "ifs" he experienced, was darkness. He ran to a place of hiding, hoping light would become dark and hide him from the very One by whom he needed to be found. But God got there first.

David hoped the day would become dark as night. And that night would obscure the gaze of the One he didn't want to know him at his worst. David found out night was not dark to God.

David's son, Solomon, took this to its logical conclusion. He inexplicably writes contrasting stories that run the "as if" scenario to two different ends.

Love and loss.

> If I say,
> "Surely the
> darkness will
> hide me and
> the light
> become night
> around me..."
> ~Psalm 139:11

75

The Sage's two powerful books are in the Wisdom Literature of the Old Testament. Each clearly illustrates one side of living with or without wonder.

First, there is Ecclesiastes. In it, the King describes **life without wonder**. He bookends his 12-chapter morose recounting of life "under the sun" with these words:

"Meaningless! Meaningless!" says the Teacher. *"Utterly meaningless! Everything is meaningless."*[1]

"Meaningless" literally means empty or useless

Living doesn't matter, because life has no meaning. Living on this planet is vain and has no real purpose. You shouldn't live with hope because life never meets expectation. You really can't find satisfaction. Solomon—the guy who did and had everything—sums up life as one immense disappointment.

As proof that life sucks, Solomon divulges a litany of things he has tried but found meaningless.[2]

- Wisdom—*"For with much wisdom comes much sorrow; the more knowledge, the more grief."*
- Pleasure—*"I denied myself nothing my eyes desired; I refused my heart no pleasure. Yet when I surveyed all that my hands had done and what I had toiled to achieve, everything was meaningless."*
- Work—*"The work that is done under the sun was grievous to me. All of it is meaningless…I hated all the things I had toiled for under the sun."*
- Faith—*"Much dreaming and many words are meaningless."*
- Wealth—*"Whoever loves money never has enough; whoever loves wealth is never satisfied with their income. This too is meaningless."*

For this wise man, life felt incredibly unjust (*"The righteous get what the wicked deserve, and the wicked get what the righteous deserve,"*) and unfair (*"as it is with the good, so with the sinful"*).

His summation is brutal. *"So I hated life… No one can comprehend what goes on under the sun. Despite all their efforts to search it out, no one can discover its meaning."*[3]

After all he had seen and experienced, this royally favored, radically blessed man concluded: life is nothing more than chasing wind.

Now contrast this dismal view with what the same King expressed in his story of a radical love with a Shulamite woman. He records the affair in a song where he describes **life with wonder.**

Song of Songs is the most excellent of all songs because you must sing true love to fully capture it. You don't talk about love like this; you sing it.

There are only two characters that matter in this story. There is the groom, and he is a King. The other is a poor girl from a nowhere town called Shulem. However, this beloved woman is a rare beauty.

> *Their love story is a progression of increasing wonder*

You see the growth, maturation and culmination of this epic love in three simple statements she makes about her lover.

The story begins with the beautiful woman so caught up with the fact that this magnificent King thinks she's beautiful that she takes a self-absorbed stance. *"My beloved is mine, and I am his: he feedeth among the lilies."*[4] IT'S ALL ABOUT ME!

But as the passionate love grows, she realizes something profound and declares it in a redefined relational understanding. *"I am my beloved's, and my beloved is mine: he feedeth among the lilies."*[5] The change is subtle, but present. Her lover now takes first place. She defines herself by his love—"I am his!" Priorities have dramatically changed so she declares, IT'S ALL ABOUT US!

But then the love story takes a dark turn. They experience disappointment and difficulty. Her dreams conflict with the King's. She faces sad moments because of her refusal to run with him. That's when he withdraws, and as she struggles to find him, she walks through the pain of loneliness and rejection.

But it's in that pain that she moves to the place where she wants nothing but to be at his side. Nothing less, nothing else. Restored relationship leads to renewed intimacy. Now she understands the place the King should have in her heart. She speaks such touching words of surrender.

"I am my beloved's, and his desire is toward me."[6] She's finally arrived at the point where she fully believes, IT'S ALL ABOUT HIM!

Surrender becomes her place of rest. *"My own vineyard is mine to give. Let us go early to the vineyards to see if the vines have budded, if their blossoms have opened, and if the pomegranates are in bloom—there I will give you my love."*[7]

The end of the love story is so moving. Because she now lived in wonder, the King was amazed and enamored with her. As she sat in awe of Him, He stood in awe of her. The conclusion they both arrive at is clear. Life is nothing less than chasing wonder.

Wonder is a sacramental mindset

It's an internal spiritual reality reflected by external physical action. *"With breathtaking wonder, let everyone worship Yahweh, this awe-inspiring Creator."*[8]

Jan Van Der Hoeven was warden of the Garden Tomb in Jerusalem—the traditional site of Jesus' burial and resurrection. He once described the response of a hippie who heard John's proclamation of the fullness of Jesus' forgiveness of sin. The Warden pointed out the magnificent contrast between Golgotha's skull-like cliff just east of the Garden, and the Tomb from which Jesus had risen.

The visiting vagabond who was in search of reality listened spellbound. As Van Der Hoeven concluded, the young man called out from the crowd, "Mister, if what you say is true, there should be singing and dancing for joy at this site every day of the year!"

That's the spirit behind Jesus' statement to which I keep returning. *"Truly I say to you, whoever does not receive the kingdom of God like a child will not enter it at all."*[9]

This is seeing *what is* as if it contains *what should be.*

IF NOT

""If not us, who? If not now, when?"
~ John F. Kennedy

In the Kingdom, anything of real value finds its source in the person and presence of God released through the Spirit of Jesus. We *receive* the life and power we need for God to move in or through us.

All we are in Him *is* all He is in us.

Look at the image Jesus uses. *"Out of your bellies…rivers of living water."*[1] Rivers are always new, always fresh, always moving, always flowing, as long as they remain connected to a perennial source.

When Jesus taught the Disciples to pray, He began with the phrase, *"Our Father."*[2] Strangely, Jesus did not use his normal paternal name for Father, *Abba.* Instead, He used *Pater,* a less intimate term referring to Father as the one who sires, the source of life—the person from whom we originate. Father here refers to the One from whom we get our identity, name, character and abilities.

> *"Even the darkness will not be dark to you; the night will shine like the day, for darkness is as light to you."*
> *~Psalm 139:12*

In the Kingdom, everything depends on receiving.
It is the single most important trait we need to be part of what God is doing. All we are and have comes from the Father.

When we reach any imposed limit on our receiving, we then limit how much God can do in, for and through us. The size of our capacity to receive is the *only* limit to the scale of His capacity to move.

Our problem in ministry is not sourcing a move, it's sustaining one. Our Source is inexhaustible. But we get frequently exhausted.

The issue is capacity.

Capacity must grow to contain and release what God wants to do in the future. We've got to stretch to contain what He gives, because we can only give what we receive. Our most significant prayer may be, "Lord, expand my capacity to receive."

> *Our capacity needs to match*
> *God's generosity*

As I write this chapter, supply chain problems are choking both individual business and the broader economy. A supply chain is simply the connecting links between an item's origin—say harvesting of a sweet potato—and the final destination for the consumer—a dinner plate. When any link fails, the entire system grinds to a halt. Delays in supply mean higher prices in the end.

Capacity is based on the strategic link between the producer and the receiver. When there is increasing demand, there is a corresponding need for increased capacity.

The Church does not currently have enough capacity to sustain what God wants to do in the future. Growth in our capacity to receive is essential to the expansion of a genuine, widespread move of God.

But honestly, we can get weary doing good—otherwise Paul wouldn't have warned us about it twice.[3] Fatigue is a weak link in our supply chain. If that connection breaks, we lose our only source of Heaven-to-earth living. This weariness comes when we run out of room for Him to fill us. The moment we arrive at the end of supply. Scraping the bottom of the tank.

Let's review a couple of pictures that help us understand this need for expanding capacity to receive.

First, Jesus encountered a woman at a dinner who anointed His feet with very expensive perfume. She broke the neck of a priceless alabaster jar and poured the perfume on Him. This woman gave Jesus extravagant worship that cost her something invaluable which she could never use again.[4]

Next, we hear of a widow whose husband had left her deeply in debt.[5] She was about to lose her sons to loan sharks when she ran to the man of God in despair. He gave her a miraculous answer—send the boys to get all the containers they could find. Then, using her little oil cruet, watch as God multiplies the source to meet the need.

A few things stand out in these stories. Both main characters were women, therefore undervalued in the culture. Each woman was shattered. One in deep debt, the other in deep sin. Both were also desperate. At the end of their ropes, with nowhere to turn.

The New Testament story of the woman with the alabaster jar is the genesis of great songs and word pictures describing an ultimate act of worship. She broke the jar, gave it all and left smelling like Jesus. What an awesome picture! But it is also limiting. While an image of our ultimate goal—to give Jesus everything—it isn't the best picture of a life of worship because when the nard was gone, there was nothing else to pour out.

For me, the Old Testament story best pictures life in Christ. The oil (Holy Spirit) never runs out as long as there is room to receive. The oil only stops when capacity ceases to grow.

Look at the command of the prophet to the widow: Get all the containers you can. Beg, borrow, steel—just *INCREASE CAPACITY* as much as you can. She knew she could sell the oil to pay for the past and provide for the future.

One thing the Prophet did not do is put a limit on the number of containers.

The mother reached a point where she said to her sons, "bring me another jar" but their response was, "there are no more." That's when the Bible notes, "***then*** the oil stopped flowing." With no limit on capacity, oil would never stop flowing. But the sons gave up on finding more vessels.

They had maximized their capacity to receive

Had they found more containers, the oil would have kept flowing. Then they would not only have enough for their own needs, there would also have been abundance to share with others who were going through the same pain. The capacity to receive defined the limits of the oil supply. Limited capacity limited impact. Restricting the spiritual dimension of Him who is for us will limit how much we impact the One who is against us.

God *ALWAYS* has more. The question is, do we possess the capacity to receive it?

The proportions of outpouring correspond to the dimensions of our reception. Jesus once said, *"with the measure you use, it will be measured to you."*[6] Luke records Him saying, *"Give and it will be given to you. A good measure, pressed down shaken together and running over will be poured into your lap. For with the measure you use, it will be measured to you."*[7]

Here is a Kingdom principle applicable across the board. We must make room for provision. Overflow, abundance, more than enough, only happens as we expand our capacity to receive. We'll always get more than we can contain, but we should also advance toward containing more.

> *There are two ways capacity increases*
> *Neither one is fun*

Pruning. In Jesus' famous parable about vines and wines, the thing that causes the branches to be most fruitful is pruning.[8] This severe cutting increases the ability to produce and improves the quality of the grapes by removing the non-essential stuff using up resources.

Poop Jesus also told this parable. *"A man had a fig tree growing in his vineyard, and he went to look for fruit on it but did not find any. So he said to the man who took care of the vineyard, 'For three years now I've been coming to look for fruit on this fig tree and haven't found any. Cut it down! Why should it use up the soil?' 'Sir,' the man replied, 'leave it alone for one more year, and I'll dig around it and fertilize it. If it bears fruit next year, fine! If not, then cut it down.'"*[9]

I love J. B. Phillips paraphrase, *"dig round it and give it a bit of manure."*

This word *"fertilized"* is actually "dung" or "manure." Oddly, it comes from a root word meaning "wail, lament, mourn." The idea behind it seems to be, all the crappy circumstances you endure contain the very nutrients your soul needs to make life fruitful. The poo infuses essential nutrient deposits for growth. Take care of the tree, fruit takes care of itself.

Everything you face must always pass through this grid of understanding in order to benefit you. The manure life deposits on us matures us from *"fruit,"* the expression of the vine distributed through the branch, to *"much fruit,"* the assorted types of productivity. It culminates with *"fruit that remains,"* those results that stand the test of time and carry forward to future generations.[10]

The incredible promise of the New Testament is that there are no limits for our capacity to receive.

We live in a generation facing a new and incredible challenge from God. Will Jesus find in this generation a people so connected to His Spirit and life that we produce fruit in and out of season? If not us, who? If not now, when?

Before Christ invested His Spirit in all His followers, God-lovers only produced fruit *"in season."* But Jesus crushed that idea when He cursed a fig tree which wasn't bearing fruit *OUT of season.*[11] Why? He understood the inexhaustible nature of the source He provided. That's why He could demand and expect fruit in *every* season.

Both Old and New Testaments contain promises about this flourishing fruit.

The wild old Prophet Ezekiel saw a river flowing from the house of God. It fed trees along its banks that bore fruit every month. This produce that did not fail was both good for food and the leaves brought healing.[12] God's ultimate design was to have people whose lives released His life all the time for the nourishment and healing of the culture.

John seems to see a similar river as he gets this amazing vision of the future. *"The angel showed me the river of the water of life, as clear as crystal, flowing from the throne of God and of the Lamb down the middle of the great street of the city. On each side of the river stood the tree of life, bearing twelve crops of fruit, yielding its fruit every month. And the leaves of the tree are for the healing of the nations."*[13] Here is the fruit that remains.

A life of wonder is a life with no limits. God's grace knows no bounds; His power has no constraints. Our capacity to receive must expand. There are no limits for those who faithfully connect to the Source of Life.

DISCOVERY

3

God Builds My Life

As His

Dream Come True

Psalm 139:13-16

For you created my inmost being; you knit me together in my mother's womb. I praise you because I am fearfully and wonderfully made; your works are wonderful, I know that full well. My frame was not hidden from you when I was made in the secret place, when I was woven together in the depths of the earth. Your eyes saw my unformed body; all the days ordained for me were written in your book before one of them came to be.

A STITCH
IN TIME

*"No matter how it looks from the outside,
everything that is made by hand requires a lifetime of effort."*
~ Kit Dunsmore

To say the season we've been through over the last couple of years has been challenging would radically understate the obvious.

The incalculable costs of a pandemic piled on top of unparalleled political and social upheaval leaves us standing at a crossroad in culture that is difficult to comprehend and impossible to explain.

Popular culture oversimplifies complex moments. The tendency is to sum up the indescribable with a watchword—a word you hear over and over until it becomes a mantra for the season.

The current buzzword is *unprecedented*.

Descriptions of the pandemic, social upheaval, racial conflict, unemployment, levels of fear, government overreach—any area we examine these days gets slapped with the moniker.

> *"For you created my inmost being; you knit me together in my mother's womb."*
> *~Psalm 139:13*

Truth is, that word captures the spirit of our day. We've just seen nothing like this before. Unprecedented encapsulates the mental and spiritual chaos surrounding us.

How do you make sense out of what you've never seen before?

It's as if someone dumped out a massive 5000-piece jigsaw puzzle on a table and we're supposed to assemble the random pieces without the picture on the front of the box. We don't know how to construct it because we don't know what it's supposed to look like when we're done.

I've been pondering how this season fits in the flow of *His*-story.

- To correctly understand what is ahead of us, we must fully grasp what is around us.
- To grasp what surrounds us, we must correctly understand what is behind us.

The meaning of what's ahead of us often gets buried in the mess of what's behind us. To see where we're going, we should remember where we've been.

Destiny most often hides in history

To see the future accurately, we look back. But we need to look back far enough. We will never understand what God really wants to do in our day if we start at the wrong beginning.

People of the Word sometimes look nostalgically back to Eden. We think the story began in a Garden. You know, Adam, Eve, trees, a serpent and the Fall. We blew it. God fixed it. For many, this sums up the good news. And it is great news, but it's also only part of the story.

A deeper question percolates as we try to make sense of unprecedented times. What was God dreaming that drove him to create in the first place?

Let's set current reality in the context of a much bigger story—the dream buried in the heart of the Father before He made one molecule of what we see around us. If we start in the Garden, we'll end up satisfied with getting redeemed and making it to Glory. That becomes our ultimate reversal—the Fall of man flipped on its head. Look only to Eden for identity, and you'll be content with getting saved and getting to heaven.

But God's dream didn't begin in Eden. What He imagined was deep in His heart long before He planted a Garden.

An End was in His heart before The Beginning.

His actual dream isn't about getting earth to Heaven. It's about getting Heaven to earth. It's not primarily about where we end up going, but what we end up being. God knit us together in our mother's womb so He could knit us into the tapestry of Glory He's creating. We are each a stitch in time.

God's commitment to destiny runs deep. We spend so much of our lives trying to persuade God to make our dreams come true. God focuses on making us His dream come true.

Paul actually explores this in his letter to the people of God at Ephesus. He writes to this power church about a mystery hidden for generations; only seen in types and shadows.

Paul understood his destiny because God chose him *"to preach to the Gentiles the boundless riches of Christ, and to make plain to everyone the administration of this mystery, which for ages past was kept hidden in God, who created all things."*[1]

There is a deep mystery behind the world we are in and life as we know it. But in the person of Jesus, the mystery is revealed. Paul unpacks this mystery of history that reveals destiny.

> *Jesus was God's dream set before us in panoramic technicolor*

God showed us what He meant for us to be when He made us. Jesus came to show us what God looks like when He looks like us. But He also showed us what we look like when we look like God.

To understand who we are and what we're designed and destined to become, we cannot let current circumstance or difficulty define us. Go back to the beginning and explore what was in God's heart before He created you. Probe questions like:

- What did God envision when he drew the blueprints of this eternal construction project called "time?"
- What was God dreaming when He scooped dirt and blew life into a mud pie called "man?"

While it's true we are in a historically unprecedented moment, let's remember we have an unprecedented God who wants to build an unprecedented people to live unprecedented lives and do unprecedented things. It's why He made everything He made!

It occurred to me as I've reviewed this pregnant period, we have the choice to live the day when God's dream comes true. So how do we participate—maybe cooperate is a better word—with God in the actualization of His dream? That's the theological cave in which Paul goes spelunking.

First, the Apostle says we must fully embrace God's dream.

"His intent was that now, through the church, the manifold wisdom of God should be made known to the rulers and authorities in the heavenly realms, according to his eternal purpose that he accomplished in Christ Jesus our Lord."[2]

God had an ultimate intention. This was the motive beneath creation and the meaning behind history from the beginning. It's what God had up His eternal sleeve all along.

His intention is intended to blow our minds!

God's desire relates to *"now,"* at this present moment, right here in the mess we're in. Not someday in Heaven, but now and from now on. It's the answer to Jesus' declarative call, *"let your kingdom come, let your will be done, on earth as it is in heaven."*[3]

The passion of God all along was to operate *"through the church"*—that's us. We are the vehicle for His intention. People have always been the way He intended to do what He meant to do. Plan A and there is no Plan B.

His goal is for the church to put on living display His *"manifold wisdom."* The word translated *"manifold"* is beautiful. It means "many colored" and refers to the intricate beauty of an embroidered pattern or the endless color variety of flowers.

We are the living proof to Heaven and earth that God knew what He was doing. This variegated glory of God in us is *"made known"*—declared and certified—to the angelic hosts in Heaven and the devilish beings in Hell.

These *"rulers and authorities"* Paul says we are schooling are the highest-ranking beings in heaven. The word is *arche*—the powers God made first.

"Authorities" are the decision makers, the course-shapers who enforce the will of God.

Remember, every time angels appear in Scripture, people are told, *"fear not."* Angels scare the bejabbers out of people! These beings are immense, impressive and intimidating. They rule celestial territories, control world events, enforce divine initiatives and intervene in personal destinies. They surround the throne of God and are the army host of Heaven.

Yet, we school them. We are angel school!

At the birth of Jesus, the shepherds wanted to see "the things made known *to us*" by their angelic visitors. But after the resurrection, the angels now want to see "the things made known to them" *through* us!

The least of the redeemed outranks the greatest of the Archangels. In our union with the death and resurrection of Jesus, we legally sit on the throne and reign with Him. We are *"seated with Christ in heavenly places."*[4] We display what Heaven looks like here and now, in our plot of earth just as it is in Heaven.

> ## What we do doesn't just impact time, it informs eternity

These heavenly beings watch in wonder at the spectacle of God's wisdom exhibited through man's weakness. It baffles me, but God designed us to humble Heaven & humiliate hell. We make Heaven sing and Hell shake.

It is illegal for us to believe we are not important to this world. We are critical, even central, to all God is doing. The Church is His chosen vehicle to display to the universe how smart He is! We manifest secrets that God reveals only in our lives, no matter how inconsistent, checkered, weak or ignorant.

Paul calls it *"God's eternal purpose in Jesus."* It is God's dream.

When both Heaven and Hell see God's people enforcing through prayer and obedience the will of God on earth in real time, it fulfills this intention. We make His dream come true. This reality should efficiently blow us away!

Only through fully redeemed human beings can the universe see the fullness of what God had in mind when He spoke Creation into being.

Paul's exhortation is simple: live the dream! Walk in the wonder.

This was so important that Paul committed deep prayer to seeing it fulfilled. *"For this reason,"* indicates that it was God's dream that drove Paul's prayer.[5]

The focus of his prayer was that we would know:[6]

- **Who we are.** Our identity comes from His paternity (*"...from whom every family in heaven and on earth derives its name,"*).
- **What we carry.** Each of us carries His Presence and fills our spheres of influence with His life (*"...out of his glorious riches he may strengthen you with power through his Spirit in your inner being, so that Christ may dwell in your hearts through faith,"*).
- **Where we belong.** Rooted and grounded in Him through our covenant connection with His people. (*"...that you, being rooted and established in love, may have power, together with all the Lord's holy people, to grasp how wide and long and high and deep is the love of Christ,"*).

When we assimilate these things, we will have the power to grasp the heart of the dream—life in His love.

Paul clearly sets the proportions of this love. *Breadth*—how big the love is. *Depth*—how far it will go. *Length*—how long it will last. *Height*—how strong it is. Knowing these dimensions of divine favor, we will become risk-takers, chain-breakers, history-makers, planet-shakers.

When we know the fulness of His love, we become the fulness of His stature...we measure up to Jesus. As full of God as God is! (*"filled to the measure of all the fullness of God,"*).[7]

When we fulfill God's original intention, it is the highest praise in creation. *"Now we offer to God all the glorious praise that rises from every church in every generation through Jesus Christ—and all that will yet be manifest through time and eternity. Amen!"*[8]

When we live at this level of wonder, we will see—we will *be*—His dream come true.

SPHERE OF INFLUENCE

"No matter how it looks from the outside,
everything that is made by hand requires a lifetime of effort."
~ Kit Dunsmore

Modern social media has done much to distort and pervert the idea of influence in culture.

An *"influencer"* today is a social media personality who establishes credibility and builds an audience with the sole focus of becoming a brand. They use personal leverage to persuade others based on a perceived trustworthiness or authenticity.

A successful influencer attracts attention and garners a following but doesn't always have anything important to deposit in those who follow them. These populist obsessions run the gamut from sports and entertainment to business and religion. Substance is optional and shallow is acceptable.

> "I praise you because I am fearfully and wonderfully made; your works are wonderful, I know that full well.
> ~Psalm 139:14

Serious issues have surfaced because we have unwittingly but willingly swallowed two complete fabrications that confuse the truth about lasting significance.

These myths have led to a tepid understanding of influence.

Myth #1:

Influence equals **IMAGE**. The prominent perception is that to be seen is to be significant. Protect your image (no matter how airbrushed and artificial) at any price because it is the currency of contemporary culture. But we forget, being visible does not equal being valuable.

Myth #2:

Influence equals **IMPRESSION**. Garnering attention and making an impression is the commodity of the internet. Get attention at any cost. But it is easy to make an impression but not make a difference.

Image and impression are about being seen no matter the result. Influence is about the result no matter if you're ever seen.

In stark contrast to the image/impression approach is authentic influence. This is the ability and capacity to create change from within a structure, system or relationship without manipulative pressure to control people.

Influence, by definition, cannot merely create lists of rules, pressure others to conform or silence the uniqueness of others. It is invasive but not intrusive. The word itself paints a picture of how influence works. The root of the word is Latin and means to flow into (*in* = into; *fluere* = to flow).

So influence, especially Godly influence, works in three ways. It infiltrates—penetrating by relationship. Informs—releasing insight and wisdom. And inflames—inspiring to action.

Influence is all about impact

Making a difference. Being a change-agent in our sphere of influence.

Influence accomplishes two critical things when administered correctly.

First, it shapes culture. As we engage the ultimate Influencer (Holy Spirit), He infects the areas of life we engage as we host and carry His presence. Second, it shifts atmosphere. Difference makers shape history because they exhibit and release God's power through love.

Everyone is an influencer. But not every influence is of equal importance.

Each follower of Christ possesses and projects Kingdom import. But this influence also has potential to increase. The more we influence the things at hand, the more God puts at hand.

Influence is the God-approach to change. It is His adaptive power working through us. People who walk in wonder seamlessly create transformation because of how and how much they stand out from the crowd. They swim upstream instead of going with the flow. They are salmon in a world of tilapia.

The two primary ways we influence is by who we are and what we carry. As we walk in the integrity of person, we find open doors to effect change by presence, power and purity.

PRESENCE

This is the primary means of Kingdom influence. We work within systems with what is within us. Our relational authority shapes our positional impact.

Jesus illustrated it beautifully with one of His Kingdom stories. *"He told them still another parable: The kingdom of heaven is like yeast that a woman took and mixed into about sixty pounds of flour until it worked all through the dough."*[1]

Any baker will tell you the power of yeast is proximity. It has to be *"hidden in"* the dough for it to work. In the world, not of the world, the Master said.

> *Incarnation was always Jesus'*
> *chosen method*

In fact, most of His parables picture the hiddenness of the Kingdom. He speaks of buried treasure, secret pearls, wheat growing among weeds. And here, yeast worked into dough.

Influence is never aloof or distant. Like the King Himself, Kingdom influencers are *a part of* not *apart from* what they desire to change. For influence to have highest impact requires the intimacy of proximity.

Being present to the place we want to affect requires adaptability. We shift approach in order to shift atmosphere.

Being fully engaged in a situation you want to impact leaves you with a:

- Key choice—I take the risk of involvement by taking a chance on relationship.
- Key challenge—I avoid the pull of distraction by staying on mission.

My sphere of influence depends completely on my degree of connection. The value I bring to a situation depends on the quality of what I release into it.

POWER

Again, Jesus paints a graphic picture for us. *"You are the salt of the earth. But if the salt loses its saltiness, how can it be made salty again? It is no longer good for anything, except to be thrown out and trampled underfoot."*[2]

Salt provides many benefits, but two primary ones illustrate influence. Salt preserves—it deters decay. Salt flavors—it enhances enjoyment. Salty Christians adjust the trajectory of the places in which God has positioned them.

> *Excellence is the saltiness is our character*

Our creativity, innovation, humility and compassion open the way for us to innovate solutions and imprint collaboration.

The Psalmist emphatically declares, *"Because of your favor on your vineyard, blessing extended to every mountain of influence. Through this flourishing vineyard mighty ones were raised up. The nations were blessed by your fruitful vineyard of Israel, all the way from the Mediterranean to the Euphrates."*[3]

Power, with all its inherent dangers, also leaves you with a:

- Key choice—I work at being better by pushing to offer my best.
- Key challenge—I refuse to settle for being adequate because of a healthy discontent with just good enough.

PURITY

We have the most powerful influence where we dare to be different. The difference we make is proportional to the difference we manifest.

Jesus once again gives us imagery to reshape our images. *"You are the light of the world. A town built on a hill cannot be hidden. Neither do people light a lamp and put it under a bowl. Instead they put it on its stand, and it gives light to everyone in the house. In the same way, let your light shine before others, that they may see your good deeds and glorify your Father in heaven."*[4]

The blessing of light is extensive. But two key aspects may be behind Jesus' picture. One is illumination—removing any trace of darkness. The other is revelation—exposing what is real.

Jesus said both, *"I am the light of the world"* and also *"you are the light of the world."*[5] The goal and essence of Kingdom influence is to be in our sphere of responsibility what Jesus was in His.

Light is best seen in darkness. Kind of makes our obsessive complaints about being in dark places look a bit silly. We are placed where we can best offer Kingdom brightness. We rise and shine where there is *"deep darkness."*[6]

Listen again to the Psalmist. *"Then the mountains of influence will be fruitful, and from your righteousness prosperity and peace will flow to all the people."*[7]

This single trait, purity of motivation and method, will leave us with the:

- Key choice—I must be ok with looking foolish as I live for destiny.
- Key challenge—I cannot crave conformity when I live from identity.

Living for influence instead of image and impression comes from a life committed to the big value differences of the Kingdom of God. We stand out from the cultural milieu through the stark Kingdom priorities of forgiveness, love, empathy and sacrifice.

Influence—the walk of wonder on the streets of daily—demands that we stand out. But we need not demand the world notice us when we do.

People of wonder make the world miss them when they're gone!

DEFINING MOMENT

"When a defining moment comes along, you define the moment,
or the moment defines you."
~ Kevin Costner

The multi-season series on the life of Jesus, *The Chosen,* has become a phenomenon few understand. Garnering a huge portion of its financial backing through crowdfunding, it has eclipsed all expectations of what an independent film project can do. It's also made Dallas Jenkins a household name.

In Episode 8 of Season 1, Jesus is talking intensely with Simon (Peter), who just can't figure out why Jesus chose Matthew—a crooked tax collector—to be part of the entourage. Peter objected, "I just don't think it's a good idea to pick him."

Jesus' classic response was, "A lot of people didn't think it was such a good idea when I picked you!" Simon indignantly replies, "But this is different."

Jesus' next words became a defining phrase for the entire series. He smiled at Simon and said...

"Get used to different."[1]

"My frame was not hidden from you
when I was made in the secret place,
when I was woven together in the depths of the earth."
~Psalm 139:15

So many people observing Jesus' life needed those words. If Jesus was anything, He was different—unlike anything they'd seen or heard. Uniquely distinct from anyone they'd ever known.

An event we celebrate annually as the triumphal entry on Palm Sunday, illustrates it so well. People who thought they could define Jesus threw the first century equivalent of a ticker tape parade. Seemed appropriate because Jesus had raised Lazarus from the dead—a huge win in the eyes of the people.

Matthew records that *"the whole city was stirred."*[2] Unparalleled crowd buzz erupted as Jesus' donkey ride exploded into a spontaneous outburst of Messianic joy. In the minds of the crowd walking with Him, Jesus was a King on his way to a coup.

It's vital to remember, Jesus did nothing by accident. He book-ended that first Palm Sunday with a two-part event that pulled back the veil to put Kingdom on display. He very much wanted His followers that day to experience His reign and to see how very different it was.

Simultaneous to Jesus' triumphal entry, there was another important event taking place across town. You might remember that when Jesus was born, Luke mentioned a bunch of Shepherds *"keeping watch over their flocks by night."*[3] Now, decades later, the shepherds tasked with those nativity sheep led that special flock of Paschal Lambs past the tower of Migdal Eder into Jerusalem. These were unblemished lambs to be chosen by families as part of their Passover Seder.

It was the last time they would ever need those lambs.

Entering on the other side of Jerusalem was the true, eternal Passover Lamb. The One John called, *"Lamb of God who takes away the sin of the world."*[4]

> *This Lamb would settle the issue of sin once and for all*

That perspective was underwriting the actions of the parade-goers escorting Jesus that Sunday. In their eyes, Messiah was heading into the Holy City to set up the Kingdom for which they'd been waiting so long. They were absolutely certain they had this whole Messiah picture figured out.

To them, this was a dream come true! They were right…sort of. Jesus was ushering in a dream, but it was God's dream, not theirs. The parade that day was neither Jesus' idea nor God's vision.

Human tendency to cast the Lord and His purpose into our paradigm is pervasive. God made us in His image and we've been trying to return the favor ever since. This perpetual habit of creating a construct and then attempting to box God into it is the root of our disappointments with God.

Disillusionment rises from illusion. That procession of Palm Sunday partiers had a serious illusion.

To be fair, Jesus did sort of incite the parade. He dispatched a couple disciples to town so they could commandeer transportation—a mama donkey and her baby, according to Matthew's account. The crowd completely missed that obvious clue. Something was seriously juxtaposed to their vision—*the donkey*.

Jesus came riding humbly on a miniature mule, not boldly on a white stallion. He was entering the city to the singing voices of children, not the drumbeat of marching armies. This was a path of palm fronds and overcoats, not a victory march with princes and overlords.

While the people missed the point during the parade, they couldn't miss it at the Temple later that day. The triumphal entry and the cleansing of the Temple are parts A & B of the same organically connected event. Both essential lessons Jesus' followers would need the rest of their lives.

This was Kingdom come

The Triumphal Entry was all about a King and a Kingdom. Despite His mode of transport, Jesus was entering the city as a King entering to clean house. But here was a King unlike any the people had imagined. He came humbly, simply, gently. Yet He still came to change everything. Jesus simply refused to be defined by the crowd's expectation.

His defining moment became ours. This historical pivot point illustrates Kingdom values that radically contradicted the values of a culture drifting without moorings. The priorities He displayed that day made up the heart and soul of Jesus' identity, underwriting both His ministry and legacy.

For those who follow Jesus, these serve as the underground feeder fueling the walk of wonder.

Bending Low to Reach High: Humility

The heart of the story starts with this telling phrase: *"They* (the two Disciples) *brought the donkey and the colt, and put their cloaks on them, and Jesus took his seat."*[5]

The New Testament often describes the ascended Savior as seated on the throne at the right hand of His Father in Heaven. But Jesus took a seat on a mule before He took His seat on the throne. He revealed that in His Kingdom to take a seat of honor, you first take a seat of humility.

Jesus chose the place of humility, even while carrying the weight of Heaven's authority. He fulfilled Zechariah's prophecy that the King of Heaven would come humbly. This was a different type of King presiding over a different kind of Kingdom. Our King came humbly. His chief weapon to disarm enemies was mercy. His most potent tool to capture human hearts was love.

During Biblical times, the way a king entered a city declared the reason he'd come. If he came for war, he entered on a horse. If he came in peace, he rode a donkey. The Triumphal entry was a "do you really trust me?" event for His followers. A defining moment of faith.

We are called to carry His authority in the earth, but authority only comes as we embrace a King who stoops low. Humility is the seat of honor in His Kingdom. A Kingdom where leaders bow to reach the least of these.

Seeing Your Reflection In Jesus' Face: Identity

Seeing the prophetic picture of Jesus playing out before them, the crowd swelled until *"an exceptionally large crowd gathered and carpeted the road before him with their cloaks and prayer shawls."*[6] Jesus rode in the center of the procession, crowds surrounded him shouting, *"Hosanna, Lord, Son of David! He comes sent from the God! We celebrate with praises to God in the highest!"*[7] This was a chorus of celebration and a cry of desperation.

"Hosanna!" is a call for help and a cry of hope; both supplication and declaration. It means both *"God save us!"* and *"God saves us!"* A consummate prayer for a future where God would come to rescue and reign.

Oddly, that shout raised a question in the crowd, *"Who is this?"* The people instinctively knew that the identity of the man on the mule defined them. Who He was determined who they were.

Unfortunately, the Jewish people had their hope rooted in memories of yesterday. What God had done, not what God was doing or going to do. Their preconceived notions of a military Messiah restricted their understanding of this guy on the donkey, *"This is the prophet Jesus, from Nazareth in Galilee."*[8]

But Jesus was a new picture of tomorrow. His Kingdom stood focused not on what earth demanded of Heaven, but on what Heaven released to earth. The crowd couldn't see the King because of the donkey. Consequently, they couldn't see themselves as citizens of this King's new Kingdom.

> *We only see ourselves as we really are*
> *when we see Jesus as He really is*

How we define Him defines us. Our view of what is real rises from our comprehension of His Kingdom as upside down to the values, priorities, atmosphere and principles of what we see around us. We will always need Jesus to show us who we really are.

Wonder is the clear evidence that I understand myself in light of who He is. That is David's whole point in this Psalm of self-revelation. God defines me.

You can't see who Jesus can be for you if you imprison Him in some previous understanding you've had of Him. Confine Jesus to who He has been in your past and you'll never see who He wants to be in your future.

Living From The Father's Heart: Mercy

Now we come to part two of Jesus' epic day. Upon entering Jerusalem, Jesus went directly into the temple area and drove away all the merchants who were buying and selling their goods. Dumping their goods on the ground, He defiantly said to them, *"My dwelling place will be known as a house of prayer, but you have made it into a hangout for thieves!"*[9] Nothing gets under Jesus' skin like people putting obstacles between hurting souls and the heart of His Father. It sends Him into an eternal fit.

God wanted to make it easy for people to get to Him. The religious bunch wanted to make it hard. They set up stalls, instituted taxes, hiked up prices and created a screening process that discouraged even the most devoted from trying to get near God.

Jesus' words and actions may feel extreme for our spiritual comfort zone, but He vehemently opposed anything or anyone who stood between the people and the Father. Jesus had a heart for the broken and heartburn with anyone that stood between them and the Father.

The expression may have been anger, but the ethos was mercy. He was defending the Father's reputation and securing His dream. Jesus won't tolerate a merciless people misrepresenting His merciful Father.

What comes next is breathtaking. *"Then the blind and the crippled came into the temple courts, and Jesus healed them all."*[10] After the religious left, there was room for the lame and blind to meet the Healer.

Walking With Eternity In View: Simplicity

Not only were the blind and lame drawn to Jesus in these moments, but so were children. Free of the trappings of religious propriety and the cynicism of life's disappointments, the little ones were full of breathtaking wonder. They couldn't help but sing, *"Blessings and praises to the Son of David!"*[11]

The reaction of the religious elite is astounding. *"When the chief priests and religious scholars heard the children shouting and saw all the wonderful miracles of healing, they were furious."*[12] (TPT) That is the insanity of religion—it's impossible to see past your junk to His miracles! Jesus answered, *"Yes, I hear them. But have you never read the Scripture, 'From the lips of children and infants you have ordained praise?'"*[13]

Religion always complicates God and muddies the river of life. Jesus made it clear that those children understood what the spiritual elite didn't. He came to simplify the way to the Father. The Old Testament prophets used to describe it as *"bringing down the mountains and raising up the valleys."*[14] Making way for God. A highway on which neither fool nor wayfarer would get lost.

Destiny hides in plain sight, but you need the eyes of a child to see it. We face defining moments every time Jesus challenges our perceptions by refusing to fit into boxes that limit Him. Our response ultimately defines us.

HE KNEW YOU WHEN

"You heard me cry long before I knew my voice."
~ A. D Posey

The hardest place to live is between the dreaming and the coming true.

You're not where you were, but you're not where you're going. The past pulls at you with regrets, the future pushes against you with uncertainty. You live in a pregnant pause where everything that's happens is behind the scenes and beyond your view.

That still space called "between" can be a lonely, desperate place. A space of mystery where there are more unanswered questions than there are unquestioned answers. It constitutes the biggest challenge to wonder.

None of us ever choose to be there. But at some point, all of us will be. These seasons of waiting are inevitable because they are essential. We live in the Kingdom parenthesis before we step into our Kingdom promise.

Reality check: no one feels it more acutely than people who are believing God for something.

"Your eyes saw my unformed body; all the days ordained for me were written in your book before one of them came to be."
~Psalm 139:16

Believing people spend a lot of time between parentheses! Lay out a request to God and believe He will do it. Then life hits the pause button.

That void—that waiting room—is where Martha and Mary found themselves at the death of their beloved brother, Lazarus.[1]

It's one of the most familiar stories in the Bible. Therein lies the problem. When we know the end of a story, it can lose its connection to the reality of our living. When Mary & Martha walked through this, they had no clue how things would turn out. Read their story with that in mind.

To grasp the headspace in which these girls were floundering, we need to understand what died with Lazarus. Cultural context provides a stark picture of what it meant for these sisters to lose their brother. Losing Lazarus meant lost security, identity and prosperity. Their brother represented protection and provision. His death was the demise of a dream that left his sisters groping in the darkness of an uncertain future.

> *The four days that Lazarus lay in the grave were frightening and overwhelming*

Nagging questions haunted the girls. Deep, probing doubts ripped at the fraying edges of their faith. All of that being true, losing their brother wasn't the worst aspect of his death. The cruelest part was when Jesus didn't show.

This was an assault on all that these two women knew of Jesus. They trusted Him implicitly. Now everything about Him came into question.

Jesus spent some of the most memorable moments of His ministry at this home away from home. It's where He went to kick back, relax and just be Jesus. He often staycayed at their house—devouring Martha's feasts, laughing with Lazarus about Peter's latest shenanigans, sharing deep spiritual conversations with Mary.

All of that now seemed far from real as the sisters faced an excruciating question: why did He not come when they needed him most? What they wanted was Jesus here in the present moment. What they had were faded memories of when He used to stop by.

Look closely at what John records: Jesus loved them, He heard them, but *stayed where He was*. They sent a distress signal. *"Jesus, the one you love is sick!"* What they got in return was a busy signal.[2]

They were totally disappointed and utterly disillusioned. Their minds haunted houses where confusion, skepticism and unbelief jumped from every corner to scare them senseless.

Maybe this hits close or sounds too familiar to you right now. Most of us have been to that place where life makes no sense because Jesus makes no appearance. Despair and doubt are like goblins that haunt our hearts in those moments.

You feel alone when…
- The doctor's diagnosis is bleak.
- Your child's life is out of control.
- There's not enough money at the end of the month.
- The pink slip comes in the company mail.
- A marriage fractures and falls apart.
- The dearly loved one dies prematurely.

In such moments, there's simply no knot at the end of your rope.

Seasons like these are when the enemy of your soul will offer logical, rational explanations that hang the fault for whatever is wrong squarely on the shoulders of the God you love. He'll accuse you of everything you've ever done wrong and blame God for everything that's ever gone wrong. He will do everything he can to drain every drop of wonder from your heart.

There is a reason the enemy haunts that space between hope and help. He remembers something we forget.

> *Jesus does miraculous things between the dreaming and the coming true*

Satan is noisy in our silent space because He knows that if we hear what God says there, it changes the outcome and shifts the atmosphere for every season that follows. It scares Satan to death when God whispers. He knows what we hear shakes Hell because it shapes you.

In the days around Lazarus' death, Jesus unveils something very different about the space called "between." Through the delay with its deferred intervention and postponed presence, Jesus was unlocking a Kingdom reality that has kept

His followers through suffering and uncertainty in every generation since Mary and Martha learned this truth.

Hidden treasure lies in haunted spaces.

I fumbled around Lazarus' dark tomb and mined some Kingdom gems. These are foundational realities rising from the unalterable goodness of God, even in the unbearable seasons of life.

Silence is Not God's Opinion of You

When we struggle with God's silence during seasons of need, we ask unanswerable questions: Why can't I hear Him? What did I do so wrong that He won't talk to me? What kind of God goes mute when I most need to hear His voice? Our answers often lead to erroneous conclusions like God is mad at me; He doesn't love me; He's fickle and unreliable.

Jesus could have gone when the sisters called. He could have healed Lazarus; he could have prevented their grief. But John records, *"He loved them **SO** He waited."*[3]

There was something His followers needed to know about Him that required the schoolroom of a dark tomb. There was more for them than met their eyes. That's so hard to hang onto when you're living in the space between.

But here's the big reality. Faithfulness to hope opens the door for God to display His sparkling glory against the dark backdrop of your pain.

"Those who hope in the Lord will renew their strength. They will soar on wings like eagles; they will run and not grow weary, they will walk and not be faint."[4]

What You See Is Not What You Get

Jesus's disciples were the hook on which He was hanging Kingdom. They required some advanced knowledge of how different the rules of His reign really were. Lazarus' death was a crucial opportunity.

It troubled the Disciples greatly when they didn't leave as soon as the sisters called. They wanted to go so Jesus could do something about Lazarus' dilemma. But the Rabbi's only instruction to them was, *"This will not end in death."*[5]

Here was a fundamental truth these future leaders were going to need the rest of their lives. Jesus was telling them, *"What you see looking at a natural level will never show you what I'm doing at a supernatural level."*

The sisters and the disciples only saw death. But Jesus saw a new quality of living. They experienced profound loss. He built fresh hope. They felt unthinkable grief. He deposited unspeakable joy. They stood at a tomb of death. But Jesus saw a womb of life.

> *Jesus always functions in a higher reality*

Looking at His delay from the horizontal plane made Jesus appear either callous or coldhearted. But Jesus doesn't operate on the horizontal plane. The panoramic view He sees is so different from the microscopic view we see.

The Chapter You're In Is Not The Whole Story

Both sisters gave Jesus the same response to His tardiness. *"If you had been here, our brother wouldn't have died."*[6] Mary and Martha couldn't see beyond the conclusion they were drawing at that moment. Jesus knew that the space in which they stood was temporary. It felt like the end but was only a chapter.

What those hurting girls couldn't comprehend was that Jesus hadn't finished the story. They were stuck in a painful chapter. Jesus was writing an alternate ending.

Jesus is both author and finisher. Don't put a period where God wants a comma. Don't write *The End* on your story until the Author is through.

Pain Is A Place Of Presence

One of the most moving verses in the Bible is also the shortest. *"Jesus wept."*[7] He was so moved with compassion for his friends that tears were the natural response—even though He already knew what He was about to do. He identified with the shattering dilemma of those haunted hearts.

Jesus felt the level of difficulty living in a sin-broken world poses to those who love Him passionately. It brought Him to tears because it was never supposed to be that way. He refused to isolate from the dark corners of life.

Compassion is always Jesus' response to brokenness. "*We have a magnificent King-Priest, Jesus Christ, the Son of God, who rose into the heavenly realm for us, and now sympathizes with us in our frailty. He understands humanity, for as a man, our magnificent King-Priest was tempted in every way just as we are, and conquered sin. So now we draw near freely and boldly to where grace is enthroned, to receive mercy's kiss and discover the grace we urgently need to strengthen us in our time of weakness.*"[8]

We can connect with Jesus at levels in our struggles that we will never know in our successes. Pain offers a place of Presence where you get to see more of God's heart and understand more of His character than anywhere else.

The Outcome Is Worth The Wait

What He calls forth from apparent death is greater than any form of life we try to make of our suffering. When Jesus releases us from a tomb, His next words are always *"Turn that guy loose!!"*

Lazarus became the reason many in Bethany believed.

"Between" is the birthing room of the stuff in our lives that will bear His image long past the days of our lives. Waiting is the space where we transition from, "God make *my* dream come true," to "God make me *your* dream come true."

We become carriers of His presence and conduits of His power. Our earthy lives take on heavenly import. God shifts the size of our impact, the scope of our influence and the scale of our legacy in the silence of "between."

Trusting God's goodness in that dark space of unanswered questions and unspeakable loss is how He creates destiny and we recover wonder.

MORE THAN
A DREAM

> "A moment of a dream lived out is worth more than
> a lifetime of dreams that were only dreamed about."
> ~ Doe Zantamata

His name was Joel. God told him stuff. Not run-of-the-mill stuff. Stuff about the future nobody else could see. He was a prophet—one of those guys in the Old Testament to whom God whispered secrets. A divine confidant.

One time, God told him how the Kingdom would work after the King showed up on our soil. He said that after the Spirit walked in the shoes of a man called Messiah, that same Spirit would fill the hearts of every man, woman and child who simply asked.

The prophecy went like this: *"And it shall come to pass afterward, that I will pour out my Spirit on all flesh; your sons and your daughters shall prophesy, your old men shall dream dreams, and your young men shall see visions."* [1]

> "How precious to me are your thoughts, God! How vast is the sum of them!"
> ~Psalm 139:17

That last phrase caught my attention. It's one of those Kingdom thoughts that seems to turn the value-system of this world on its head. Old men dreaming dreams; young men seeing visions. Seems backwards to me.

111

Visions are seeing what we believe can be. We see the reality of a preferable future in which we can take part. Vision is short-term. Dreams are seeing what we never believed could be. Something so big we know it's farther than our reach and longer than our generation. Dreaming is long-range.

If my understanding is correct, it would seem old men would see visions because they don't have much time left. Young men would dream the big dreams because they had years to pursue them. But that's not what God told Joel.

God showed the prophet a Kingdom completely different from anything he'd ever imagined. A Kingdom to be birthed in a stable; its King asleep in a manger. Heaven entering earth unnoticed. Unceremoniously unsung. A tiny baby ushering in God's dream, *"on earth as it is in Heaven."*[2]

Luke records a snippet of the nativity narrative involving two people who met this Baby at only eight days old.[3] An old man and even older woman who lived Kingdom come before it ever came. Simeon and Anna were old ones who dreamed dreams. For a very long time. These were the first of a breed of people willing to see a Kingdom that was bigger than their lives, lasted longer than their days and reached farther than the eye could see.

They possessed a mature wonder with plenty of years ripening.

You might say these two old folks were waiting prophetically. A bit of an oxymoron, isn't it? Waiting is about us doing a whole lot of nothing. Prophecy is about God doing a whole lot of everything. But in the Kingdom, those two concepts interface.

> *Waiting needs prophecy,*
> *prophecy demands waiting*

So much of these nativity octogenarians' lives centered on dreams not yet come true. They were pregnant with the promise of God, but gestation was taking forever! Yet, in the frustrating madness of the wait, they never lost touch with that prophetic dream. They never surrendered wonder.

God would come to His people. God living in the neighborhood. King of Kings as next-door neighbor.

Time wears on a dream. *"Hope deferred often makes the heart sick,"*[4] says the Sage. Longing frays the soul's edges; promise pulls at those loose threads in the mind. The interlude called waiting makes the interruption called prophecy lose its urgent voice.

Seeing the Kingdom in the dark takes a different mindset. Maybe, a different "heartset." Again, Jesus called this state of heart "childlike"—*"unless you become as a little child you can't see the Kingdom of Heaven."*[5]

Let's open the backstory of these geriatric dreamers.

The requirement of all Jewish parents was to present their firstborn male child to God and "ransom" the baby back. Normally by the sacrifice of a lamb. For poorer families, two doves or pigeons were sufficient. That's what Mary and Joseph brought when they ran into these two *imagineers*.

They first encountered Simeon, a good and devout man said to be *"full of the Spirit."*[6] He constantly hung around the Temple sleuthing for God. We don't know how old he was, but he'd had more than a few laps around the sun. Each one spent *"waiting for the consolation of Israel"*[7]— the really big God-dream.

Next, there was Anna. Luke calls her *"very old."*[8] (When the Bible calls you old, you're old. When it says you're very old, that's a whole different kind of old!) She seems to have been somewhere between 95 and 105 years old. What we know for certain is that she'd spent upwards of eight decades worshipping, fasting, praying and waiting. Waiting in hope for what few dared dreamed.

There is one simple trait that sets these two dreamers apart. It's the difference between waiting pointlessly and waiting prophetically. Openness.

Dreamers live under an open Heaven

To see what everyone around them seemed to miss, they needed to live in complete vulnerability to God. Dreaming with eyes wide open. Looking farther than the eye can see. Spotting God as He snuck up on us!

Isaiah had famously prayed, *"Oh, that you would rend the heavens and come down."*[9] God had answered that petition! He ripped open the Heavens and promptly took up residence in the little town of Bethlehem.

But Heaven opened accomplishes nothing if earth is closed. To receive what's offered by an open Heaven requires some specific traits.

OPEN EYES: LOOKING FOR THE KINGDOM

An old hymn says it this way: "Watching and waiting; looking above."[10] That's how these two lived for a very long time. Watching for the promise of God to be realized. Waiting for the purpose of God to be actualized.

The word "waiting" means to take hold of and draw near to welcome. They were not only expecting, but they had a nursery ready for when Promise came to them!

They fed the fire of this hope by living in God's presence. It's what helped them both hang onto the fact that they would see God's promise no matter how long they had to wait.

OPEN EARS: LISTENING FOR THE SPIRIT

They were both listening to God's desires. Holy Spirit revealed to them they would see this dream come true. They lived receptive and responsive to Holy Spirit's promptings. Luke notes, *"moved by the Spirit,"*[11] they walked sensitive to His timing.

They could see both the place and space where God wanted to do the impossible.

OPEN MIND: LONGING FOR WHAT MATTERS

Both Simeon and Anna embraced God's plan, no matter how it looked. These teenaged parents bringing the offerings of the poor certainly didn't look like Kingdom come. That's why everyone else missed it.

But not these two. Years of waiting had trained them in the unique ways God moved. As soon as Simeon saw the baby, he knew. He took the infant in his arms and praised God. Anna also sang and praised when she held Messiah disguised as an infant.

They saw light because God had trained their eyes in the dark. Their minds were not closed. They engaged God's passion no matter who it involved or how it looked. Ordinary did not scare them away from expecting extraordinary.

OPEN HEART: LOVING FOR THE LONG HAUL

The one sad moment of these proceedings was when Simeon described the cost of the dream. When he saw the eternal reality, he declared, *"This child is destined!"*[12] That destiny would:

- Change hearts—*"cause the falling and rising of many in Israel."*
- Confront beliefs—*"a sign that will be spoken against."*
- Challenge attitudes—*"the thoughts of many hearts will be revealed."*

But Simeon could also see that dream come true is often painful. To the overwhelmed young mother he prophesied, *"a sword will pierce your own soul too."*

Seizing the reality that God dreamed you up before He cooked you up in your mother's womb is critical to walking in wonder. Hanging on to that dream requires a fortitude that refuses to settle for anything less. It takes effort to live on the edge of God's "suddenlies."

Hold on to hope in the face of despair no matter how long it takes. Keep your eyes open to see His fingerprints no matter how hard it seems. Walk in His presence no matter how much it costs.

The satisfaction of the coming true is well worth the strain of the dreaming.

LOST IN WONDER

"We carry within us the wonders we seek around us."
~Sir Thomas Browne

To live alive, really alive—not just existing, getting by or going through the motions—requires a visceral sense of wonder.

God did not create us to get by, get through, get stuff and get old. He made us for the breathless adventure of chasing His heart. Only the Kingdom of Heaven is large enough to give us that sense and make it last more than a few minutes! Anything less is simply a substitute transcendency.

As I alluded to, I've logged well over a million flight miles in my work over the last 20-plus years. The result is I've seen about every flight magazine in the business. Most of them are pretty boring, but I do have a favorite piece.

"Were I to count them,
they would
outnumber the
grains of sand—
when I awake,
I am still with
you."
~Psalm 139:18

It's a single page I always look at first in the periodical of my preferred airline. It's called, "What's In My Bag?" [1] The article pulls back the curtain on what famous people say they could never travel without.

I am usually intrigued, always amused and sometimes appalled at what travelers believed they absolutely, positively have to have to make a journey. Some are frivolous, some inane and others ridiculous. But to these spoiled trekkers, they are travel essentials.

On the journey we now call Exodus, God brought Moses and the Israelites to a critical point where they had to choose their travel essentials.[2] After the crazy cow incident, the Israelites were at a standstill of paralyzed progress. The Promised Land seemed a far-off fantasy. They derailed the dream train by attempting to accomplish God's plan their own way. At this point, they were stuck. The living moments experienced on the mountain of God turned into a dead end on their journey home.

They became short-sighted, took short-cuts and now the journey was short-circuited.

Moses came thundering down the mountain, breathing fire and tossing the divinely etched plates at their idol. The people then confronted an inescapable choice as they moved toward dream come true.

> *Is the dream of God more important than the God of the dream?*

They faced the choice of moving on with or without God's immediate, tangible presence. Was His manifest presence an essential to their journey? God would let them walk without Him if they chose to. He would allow them to do it their way. But that choice meant they were on their own.

Moses was emphatically unwilling to do that. He would not move without the guiding, intimate presence of the God who had brought them so far. He refused to climb a ladder if it was leaning against the wrong wall!

Moses' travel essentials were simple. He required the intimate presence of God, the intentional purpose of God and the intense power of God. Nothing else, nothing less.

He would not leave home without them!

It is all too easy to have success without significance; to get things done right without getting the right things done. We sometimes stand at crossroads where we must determine what is essential for us to move ahead. Then we jettison everything else.

Passion for God underwrites wonder in God. There is nothing more absolute to our finding and thriving in the Kingdom than hunger for Him. David unearthed his passion by thinking about God's heart toward him. He couldn't even number the thoughts of God toward him on any given day.

It lit such a flame in him, that he would constantly sing, *"One thing I ask from the Lord, this only do I seek: that I may dwell in the house of the Lord all the days of my life, to gaze on the beauty of the Lord and to seek him in his temple."*[3]

Wonder evacuates the heart whenever God escapes the affections.

Looking at Moses' absolute refusal to move toward the dream of God without the God of that dream has taught me a few lessons about the connection between wonder and a passion for God. I need a fire in my belly to face the fire in the desert.

Passion For God Sets Priorities In Life

The hunger I have for God determines at what level I will settle, and at which point I will stop short.

God promised the Israelites everything they wanted, everything they needed, and everything they asked for. The caveat was they would have it all without His presence. But having it all means nothing if you don't have what matters.

God refused to go with them because they were *"stiff-necked."* The word means dense or stubborn. They couldn't turn their heads, so they couldn't change their minds. If God couldn't shake their thinking, He couldn't shape their destiny. Reaching your destination means little if you miss your destiny.

A stubbornly inflexible mindset only sees how things are, not how they should be. Such obstinance kills relationship. God wants more than performance. He wants relationship. He will not move unless He has our hearts.

I need to ask myself frequently, "What is so valuable to me that my heart will break if I don't have it?" That's my driving passion. My level of passion dictates what I will do to have more. Nothing less than single-minded pursuit of His presence will get me to my place of purpose.

The Israelites ultimately understood that being successful in this world without the quest for intimacy with God is ultimately failure. They stopped worrying about their image and started thinking about their reality. Letting go of the desire to impress people let them focus on embracing God.

God's *"distressing words"* broke their hearts so that they *"began to mourn."*[4] They took a hard look at what creates distance with God and realized they broke His heart when they broke His covenant. Their sorrow created holy desperation, the first step in regaining the passion that drives wonder. What they did next in the story is so moving.

In a corporate act of repentance, these wanderers stripped off their *"ornaments."* They laid aside the false definitions of value and significance, dropped the shallow facade of false identity and confronted the reality of their deep stubbornness.

> *The things that define my priorities*
> *ultimately define my person*

Seeing their response to failure has raised some questions for me.

- What matters so much that I will change my pattern of living to get it?
- What patterns and routines of daily life will I alter for more of God?
- What stuff that I love most will I lay aside to have what I need the most?

Intimacy With God Shapes Impact In Life

The crisis at the bottom of God's Mountain showed the people of God that they needed a love worth dying for to make life worth living. God desires intimacy with His people. That requires vulnerability on our part. Only that kind of transparent relationship allows Him to disclose His plan, purpose and power.

The living example was right in front of the Israelites all the time. God spoke to Moses as a friend. Intimately, face-to-face. Moses would then return to camp prepared to handle the demands of life and leadership. His prayers impacted people and influenced God. The nation learned to pray and worship watching him. The presence of God imprinted significance on their psyche.

We don't reserve such intimacy merely for those we deem great in the Kingdom. The Psalmist promised, *"God confides in those who fear him."*[5]

Worship begets worship. Prayer releases prayer. Faithfulness inspires faithfulness.

There is a direct correlation between the impact you have on others and your intimacy with God. The legacy you leave to others is directly tied to the deposits God makes in you.

> *The more you are with God*
> *the more you are for people*

Another important note. Joshua learned to live in the Presence by watching Moses. A person who knows God intimately will always mark the next generation.

Submission To God Sculpts Significance In Life

At the mountain, these struggling stragglers found a reason to go all-in so they could go all-out. Moses prayed that he could learn how to walk in God's ways. His words were something like, *"teach me to pursue the paths of Your heart."*[6] Take me to the depths of your desires, so I can know you.

He modeled surrender to the people so they could see how its connected to understanding the voice of God.

Honestly wrestling with how things are cuts the kindling required to restart a flame for God in the heart. God can handle authentic and passionate gushings from our hearts—even if they are broken. Wrestle long enough, go deep enough, and the questions will no longer demand answers because you implicitly believe:

- God is good to me.
- God knows best for me.
- God is on my side.
- God unconditionally loves me.

Moses understood that significance for the Israelites rested solely in the manifest presence of God among them.

That's what distinguished them from all the other nations around them. It's what made them different.

God created us for presence-based living. He built into us the capacity to contain everything Jesus was, did, cared about and died for. When we choose to walk in this kind of presence, surrendered to all God wants, we choose to walk in favor, pleasure and rest. The telltale signs of wonder.

Moses' famous prayer, *"Show me your glory,"*[7] is a heart cry to see and then display who God is and what He's like. Moses was unsatisfied with living life on a horizontal plane. He wanted to experience life where God had unquestioned freedom to be who He was.

Jesus was the answer to that prayer once-and-for-all.

DISCOVERY

God Will Never

Leave

Well Enough Alone

Psalm 139:17-24

How precious to me are your thoughts, God! How vast is the sum of them! Were I to count them, they would outnumber the grains of sand—when I awake, I am still with you. If only you, God, would slay the wicked! Away from me, you who are bloodthirsty! They speak of you with evil intent; your adversaries misuse your name. Do I not hate those who hate you, Lord, and abhor those who are in rebellion against you? I have nothing but hatred for them; I count them my enemies. Search me, God, and know my heart; test me and know my anxious thoughts. See if there is any offensive way in me, and lead me in the way everlasting.

STARK CONTRAST

"Only by contact with evil could I have learned to feel by contrast the beauty of truth and love and goodness."
~ Helen Keller

Rocky Balboa was never supposed to be a contender. Apollo Creed simply needed an opponent who would get some attention but wouldn't pose a challenge. The champion picked Rocky mostly as a publicity stunt because he was from Philadelphia and had a cool nickname, "The Italian Stallion."

Nobody expected the street brawler to make any kind of showing against such a polished fighter. Ultimately, Rocky didn't even care about winning. He just wanted to go the distance. And he did. Balboa was still standing after fifteen rounds against Creed.

At one crucial moment in the final round, Creed knocked the Stallion down. Mickey, his indomitable trainer, screamed at him, "Down! Down! Stay down!" Creed danced around the ring, arms already raised in victory.

> "If only you, God, would slay the wicked!
> Away from me, you who are bloodthirsty!
> ~Psalm 139:19

Against all odds, Rocky refused to quit. He scraped himself off the mat, staggering but standing. The disbelief on Creed's face spoke volumes as Rocky rose from the canvas.

When the final bell sounded, Balboa didn't even wait to hear the announcement of who won. Jumping and celebrating, he shouted over the roar of the crowd for his darling Adrian.

Apollo won the fight, but Rocky got the girl.

The season of Covid pandemic, with all its related and unrelated chaos, has left a lot of folks knocked down and very nearly knocked out. The world, the flesh and the devil seem to all be screaming, "Stay down!"

I am convinced God is searching for a people who rise from adversity with the dogged determination of The Stallion and through their pain shout defiantly at the enemy, "Is that all you got?!" Satan really hates it when we get up. But it is glorious to see his befuddled face as he groans, "Have I got to deal with you again?"

For reasons that only make sense in Heaven, God chooses to do much of what He wants to accomplish on earth through the quite imperfect vehicle of people. He longs to make my life about more than me. God's dream for His people is partnership.

No matter where I am in the scope of my living, there is always further to go and more to become. God doesn't stop with good enough.

Abraham is a classic example. His story is one of an impossible promise, interminable waiting and unbelievable miracles. The promise and miracle part were amazing. The waiting, not so much. But it was in the pause that God shaped Abraham into a person strong enough to believe the promise but broken enough to carry the miracle.

One thing sustained Abraham between promise and fulfillment. It was the primary thing God was testing and toughening through the waiting. A quarter century passed between the time he received the initial promise (*"I'll make you a great nation of people and bless the world through you,"*[2]) and when Isaac finally made his appearance.[3] By that time, Abraham is 100 and Sarah over 90! Not exactly prime targets for a newborn.

What was it that provided light through the dark days of waiting? What kept them believing when every fact clearly opposed the dream? How could two people so doggedly hang on to a word for so long?

Hope.

"Against all hope, Abraham in hope believed and so became the father of nations."[4] The original text is even more expressive. *"Without hope, he had hope anyhow."* Translators struggle to bring out its full meaning. *"When everything was hopeless, Abraham believed anyway."*[5] *"Abraham, when hope was dead within him, went on hoping in faith."*[6]

Hope clings to promise in paradox

Biblical hope is the single trait we possess which allows us to partner with God in His purpose on earth. People of hope are people whom God can use. Hope is the foundational reality that enables God to do eternal things through earthy people. It is the portal through which *"on earth as in Heaven"*[7] passes.

This is a critical understanding because hope is the jet fuel for wonder.

So how did Abraham hope against all hope? How do we? The story offers some simple and challenging ways to hold on to the hope that lets us partner with Father's heart.

Abraham *Faithed* The Facts

Disclaimer! I am not saying we don't deal in reality. People who follow God in faith should be the most authentic to the rub and reality of life as it is. We believe God works miracles in messes, so we don't ignore the mess. We don't need to live in denial to help God do a great work.

Faithing the facts isn't the same as giving them influence—which many of us do when we simply *face* them. To Abraham, this was a God-problem. Neither he nor Sarah had physical capacity to fulfill the purpose. They were not sufficient for the promise. The Patriarch just *"didn't focus on his own impotence."*[8]

As one translator says, *"but he decided to live not on the basis of what he saw he couldn't do but on what God said he would do."*[9] He refused to allow circumstance to dictate the capacity of God. If God gave vision, He would also give provision. Hope like that has incredible power to shape the future.

Paul believed that so much, he made it the basis for an Apostolic prayer.

> *"I pray that the eyes of your heart may be enlightened in order that you may know the hope to which he has called you, the riches of his glorious*

inheritance in his holy people, and his incomparably great power for us who believe. That power is the same as the mighty strength he exerted when he raised Christ from the dead and seated him at his right hand in the heavenly realms, far above all rule and authority, power and dominion, and every name that is invoked, not only in the present age but also in the one to come. And God placed all things under his feet and appointed him to be head over everything for the church, which is his body, the fullness of him who fills everything in every way. "[10]

I am gripped by a single phrase in Abraham's story. *"Abraham believed so he became."* [11] He believed a promise and became its fulfillment. *Faith* turned him into what *fact* said he could not become. You don't have to fake it if you faith it!

Abraham Stood His Ground

Scripture says, *"He did not waver through unbelief."* [12] Honestly, that seems far-fetched. Abraham nearly gave his wife away twice! Seems like that's wavering. I think the King James gets the essence of this right, *"he staggered not at the promise of God."* That is more to the point. When God gave him what appeared to be an absurd promise, Abraham didn't stagger back in an unbelief based on his own frailty.

He accepted God as the only possible One who could fulfill His word. So the Patriarch, *"was strengthened in his faith."* The strength of his faith was God's doing. *"And gave glory to God."* [13] That part was up to him. Abraham was first *called* "father", then *became* a father. All because he dared to trust God to do what only God could do—raise the dead to life and with a word, make something out of nothing.

Abraham Trusted His Promise

Beyond and against all logic, Abraham *"remained absolutely convinced that God was able to implement his own promise."* [14] Abraham's trust in God's character was even more absolute than his faith in God's promise.

Eugene Peterson says it this way, *"He plunged into the promise."* [15] Abraham took the leap of faith and did a deep dive into the unfaltering faithfulness of God. He lived his life based on promised sufficiency, not present deficiency.

The Patriarch was a study in contrast. At times he was impatient, impulsive and impudent. Sensitive to God's voice in one moment, and in the next, he was dumb as a hammer. But along the way, he learned the central lesson that changed him from a good father (Abram) to the father of nations (Abraham).

He discovered the potent connection between waiting and hope.

Isaiah's most famous words start like this: *"They that **wait** upon the Lord."*[16] Most translators render it, *"Those who **hope** in the Lord."* So which is it? Wait or hope? Yes!

We wait in hope and hope in the wait

The Hebrew word translated, *"wait"* is a word picture. It portrays weaving or binding a cord. Making a rope. While we wait, we are weaving a rope on which we can hang our hope. Hope on a rope!

I thought about the strands we might use to braid this hope rope. We lace together the promise of God and the experience of life. Where the two meet, we create a testimony. Such testimony is the tensile strength of our hope. The places we've seen God move in our lives forge an anvil of truth on which we pound out faith when life goes wild.

The author of Hebrews says it this way: *"We who have fled to take hold of the hope set before us may be greatly encouraged. We have this hope as an anchor for the soul, firm and secure. It enters the inner sanctuary behind the curtain, where our forerunner, Jesus, has entered on our behalf."*[17]

If I attach too firmly to the overblown benefits of the temporary, I am robbed of the overarching blessings of the eternal.

Part of the purpose of these Old Testament biographies is to increase our scope of experience and understanding by showing the larger picture of His-story. By them, I am driven to the unchanging character of my God rather than the unexplainable changes of my life.

God is good despite my questions. I can cling to His love even when I cannot explain His ways. God is great in the face of my limitations. I trust Him when I can't understand Him.

This kind of bright faith is why we stand in stark contrast to the bleak hopelessness in our surrounding culture. It is the stance of wonder.

ALTAR EGOS

"Wherever an altar is found, there civilization exists."
~ Joseph de Maistre

Entering the Vortex Tunnel with our two grandsons was an experience for which I was not at all prepared. The tunnel is a virtual, mystifying, spinning, and sloping experience that leaves you walking weird for a while!

The power of this amusement is the visual illusion of movement it creates that confuses the human brain sensors. The combination of flashing and spinning lights creates the feeling that the tunnel is moving—a feeling that has you grabbing for anything that will help you stay upright.

You trust your eyes more than any other part of your body. The brain depends on eye signals to interpret reality. So when the eyes create a sensation of movement, even when nothing is moving, the brain reacts with effects that are inescapable.

In the short span of that moving hallway, I quickly lost balance, got dizzy, felt queasy and desperately floundered for something to keep me from losing my balance.

The grandsons loved it. Me?

Not so much.

"They speak of you with evil intent; your adversaries misuse your name."
~Psalm 139:20

The crazy thing is this: nothing was actually moving. The way I was seeing influenced both what I was sensing and how I was walking. An apparent reality that wasn't actually real skewed my perspective completely.

That experience got me thinking. There are two capacity-limiters that occur in the human mind. Being narrow-minded or double-minded. Both word pictures are vivid illustrations of a principle: the way we see distorts the way we think.

What we see determines how we walk

David's baptism of wonder, so beautifully described in the first two-thirds of Psalm 139, leads him to understand how and why God made him. Slowly, David adopts God's point of view. He came to feel like God did about stuff that stole the joy of wonder from the people around him.

Unless we authentically embrace God's ultimate intention for our lives, we will continually see things only on a horizontal plane. But the vertical plane—from Heaven to earth thinking—is the only way we make sense of life as it is and move toward life as it should be.

"In the beginning"[1] God had a dream. He spoke a perfect, ever-expanding universe into existence. Then, with his own hands, dug out of its soil a being who would bear his unique image. He called His creation *"man."* From that living soul, he created a companion. Man, seeing this perfect partner, called her "woman." From their union was to rise the generations that would populate this perfect world.

God desired these beings to live in His world, experiencing the same atmosphere of perfect love existing within the Trinity itself. It's as if in the counsel of eternity, the Trinity not only said, *"Let us make man in our image and after our likeness,"* but also, *"let's invite this couple into the circle of our relationship."*[2]

Freedom is the specific atmosphere in which man best grows and reaches fulfillment. Freedom just like the flow of love within the Godhead.

God encouraged Adam: *"You are free to eat from any tree in the garden..."* His only prohibition—the single limitation on man's absolute freedom—was, *"you must not eat from the tree of the knowledge of good and evil, for when you eat from it you will certainly die."*[3]

This was the prototype of the ultimate Kingdom value: live free within the atmosphere of God's presence and don't settle for anything else or anything less.

The word *"free"* in the Old Testament Hebrew is unique. We best translate it, *"unhidden"* or *"unmasked."* Freedom is the ability to live without masks, fronts, image or veneer. Ultimately, it's the undiluted realization and unfiltered expression of precisely who God designed and destined you to be.

Adam and Eve were *"naked"* in this freedom. Here's another amazing word which means *"un-crafty"* or *"un-wily."* Sure, this means unclothed, but even more that they were un-imaged and un-polished. Simply themselves; no retouching allowed. Living freely in God's presence, they needed no masks. Cover, image and facade were useless.

In God's dream for man, there was no room for shame. Even in their naked condition, Adam and Eve *"felt no shame."*[4] God didn't fit humans for masks. God never wanted to see man wearing an image that was inaccurate, inadequate or inappropriate. Pretense and posturing are as out of place in the Kingdom as a sumo wrestler at an anorexia convention!

We thrive in the atmosphere of undisguised freedom because we look most like God when we live free. It also brings the greatest glory to God as we revel in that liberty.

As the Creation narrative turns dark, it portrays the Snake as *"more crafty"* than anything else in creation. In Hebrew, the word is the exact opposite of *"naked."*[5] Unlike our primary parents, who were naked and unashamed, Satan was shrewd and slimy. The ultimate image-shaping and mask-wearing deceiver.

Using his innate cunning, the serpent seduces the couple into accessing the one thing they were told to leave alone. They misused freedom to deflect glory from God to self. Sin captured them and incarcerates us still.

> *They took a selfie and excluded God*
> *from the picture!*

The stifling atmosphere of shame entered paradise simply because they misunderstood the character of God. They believed the lie that God was not good and was not for them. Therefore, they chose to no longer trust Him.

A choice that devolved God's dream into a nightmare.

Embracing that deception about God meant Adam and Eve no longer knew the truth about themselves. They believed a lie about themselves and became the lie they believed. The moment they ate, they were aware of failure. Shame blanketed the Garden like a toxic fog. The word *shame* means, "to pale from fear; have color drain from you; to fade into the shadows."

Shame introduced loss—something God never intended for these two to experience. They immediately encountered:

- Loss of purpose—they no longer knew why they were here.
- Loss of hope—they no longer trusted the God who loved them.
- Loss of dignity—they no longer carried self-respect.
- Loss of clarity—they no longer saw reality as it was.
- Loss of integrity—they no longer lived aligned to their purpose.

Their primal reaction to such exposure was to hide from the very One who most loved them. God did not design or destine our first parents to inhabit such a broken world. They became strangers to their own environment.

> *Adam and Eve were no longer at home*
> *in the very place made for them*

Eden was not so much a place as a presence. To this day, we keep trying to get back to a place when what we are looking for is a Presence. God wanted Adam and Eve to live in Freedom. Their choice to play at designing their own destiny plunged all creation into a cycle of shame that expands and deepens to this moment.

Millennia later, we continue to drift from our original design. We're born into a severe tension—made for more, we live for less in an artificial world where we try everything to be anything but what He intended us to be.

It's what happens when we try to live apart from wonder.

We breathe the same atmosphere sin spoiled. We hide from God and each other, occupying a virtual reality through a projected image. Concerned with being attractive or acceptable—instead of authentic.

God once walked intimately with man. Together they breathed the atmosphere of Heaven. But the Fall shattered that communion.

God's intimate walk now became a desperate search. When He called them from hiding, He posed two questions we still must answer.

"Where are you?"[6] What world have you made for yourself outside my presence?

Adam's response is so insightful.[7]

- *"I heard your voice."*
- *"I was afraid."*
- *"I hid."*
- *"I was naked."*

Clearly, Adam no longer saw as God did. This duo stood pitifully covered in the fig leaves of their *alter egos.*

God's second question, *"Who told you?"*[8] was an accusation, really.

Someone redefined you

Where did you get this distorted view of who you really are? Was it abuse or abandonment as a child? Or the spouse who rejected and walked out on you? Did it rise from the addiction that hooked you in your teens? Perhaps the compulsive perfectionism or public persona you adopted to succeed and survive?

In Eden, God confronted the satanic source head on. He cursed the distortions, exposed the brokenness and declared the remedy. Killing an animal to make covers for the couple predicated centuries of altars to come. Places where animal sacrifice would change the trajectory of sinful people. That moment in the Garden was where Adam and Even discovered their *altar egos.*

Such altars became hints of restored wonder.

God expelled Adam and Eve from the Garden because shame cannot exist in the presence of God's love. When He expelled them, He was saying, "if you eat of this tree of life, you will be forever trapped in the shame that is shaping you now."[9]

God would have none of that. He made man for freedom and free man would be!

At that very moment when God blocked the way to the tree of life, He already had another Tree in mind. He prophesied to Adam and Eve the difference between the tree by which they lost everything and the tree by which more would be restored.

It might have sounded something like this:

- This tree traps you forever in your broken state,
    but that Tree sets you free forever.
- This tree seals your fate apart from Me,
    but that Tree opens the way back to my heart.
- This tree leaves you a homeless prodigal,
    but that Tree carries you all the way home.
- This tree forces you die under Law,
    but that Tree allows you to live under grace.
- This tree locks you in failure and loss,
    but that Tree liberates you in healing and abundance.
- This tree binds you to distorted identity,
    but that Tree restores you to divine intention.

God blocked the way to the Tree of the Garden so that He could open the way to the Tree of Golgotha. What a wonder!

Dietrich Bonhoeffer speaks of this beautifully. "You can hide nothing from God. The mask you wear before men will do you no good before Him. He wants to see you as you are. He wants to be gracious to you. You do not have to go on lying to yourself and your brothers, as if you were without sin; you can dare to be a sinner. Thank God for that."[10]

When we lay down our alter egos, we stand up in our *altar*ed ones.

THE GOOD FIGHT

―――――――――― ∽ ――――――――――

"You are living in a Love Story
that is set in the midst of a terrible war."
~John Eldredge

――――――― ∽ ―――――――

There is a massive difference between living with a leak and living in overflow. A leak results from some damage to the soul that allows life to escape without purpose. Overflow happens when we are so full that any time life bumps us, no matter how hard, what is in us sloshes on all those around us.

Life—and the enemy of our soul—has an incredible capacity to damage our souls and drain us of wonder. God stands firmly against anything that in that way robs us of life!

Jesus clarified beyond doubt that the only purpose of the enemy is to siphon our wonder. *"A thief has only one thing in mind—he wants to steal, slaughter, and destroy."*[1] The goal of all satanic opposition in our lives is to steal intimacy, slaughter identity and destroy destiny.

Satan is obsessed with causing leaks.

But the Master made it clear He had a far different purpose. *"But* (in contrast to the enemy's aim) *I*

> *"Do I not hate those who hate you, Lord, and abhor those who are in rebellion against you?"*
> *~Psalm 139:21*

*have come to give you everything in abundance, more than you expect—life in its fullness **until you overflow!**"*[2]

Jesus is consumed with overflow.

When we live in wonder, we learn to hate what the enemy does to people of the Dream. Simply, we were made people of the Dream not the lie. Seeing people under the influence of the lie stirs a zealous rage against the enemy of our souls. When David came to understand and embrace the thoughts of God, he stepped into that place of hating what God hates and loving what God loves.

> *You can't love what is right without hating what is wrong*

Wonder is such a militant stance. It simply refuses to accept things as they are when the as-they-should-be of Heaven is available. When we live in the Kingdom's native atmosphere of amazement and awe, we allow people who are living under the lie to see the Dream, opening their eyes to look for more.

Why is this so important at this moment? Because wonder creates the atmosphere for wonders. People of wonder invite the God of wonders to do the kind of wonders that increase the atmosphere of wonder which makes unbelievers wonder how to get in on that wonder!!

This isn't pie-in-the-sky. It is not some unrealistic panacea that approaches the pain of life with ostrich-like denial. This wonder-creating life has happened before in real time and real history.

Luke recorded it as the book of Acts! Here is an endless procession of wonders that made people wonder. The bit we need to grasp is Luke is simply describing normal life for people of wonder.

The first narrative Luke relates after the outpouring on the Day of Pentecost is the miraculous healing of a man lame from birth.[3]

Peter and John were walking in a fulness of the Spirit that brought the Kingdom so "at hand" that it affected everything they touched. They became carriers of His presence and conduits of His power.

We can learn a lot about living in wonder from this incredible story.

WONDER EXPECTS MIRACLES IN THE DAILY

The account begins with the Disciples living their daily routine. Nothing unusual or out of the ordinary.

Sometimes we get so enamored by the high-octane descriptions of miraculous movements in the ancient church that we lose touch with reality. These people lived normal lives. They walked in the mundane dailiness of life, just like we do.

The most potent thing about Acts is that the miraculous wow factor developed in the natural flow of life. We can't afford to divorce that truth from our reality.

At this point in the narrative, though, one thing had changed in these guys who just days before were hiding behind locked doors in fear for their lives. Now, a passion for presence underwrote their routine. They did the things they'd done before—like going to the Temple at the hour of prayer—but with a completely transformed heart.

Opportunities for the God of wonders to do indescribable things are everywhere, all the time. When we seek Him, we see them. Peter and John were walking the same steps as before, but because of the encounter they'd had with Holy Spirit, they were walking the same steps a different way.

This lame man—crippled since birth—was there at the Gate Beautiful every day. Doubtless, the disciples had seen him before. Perhaps, with hearts tenderized by Jesus' example, they had even given him alms. It may well be that Jesus himself passed this same beggar occasionally without taking action.

Could it be that He was leaving obvious opportunities for His friends?

Now we see the same routine with a very different outcome. What changed was the disciples. Something radically altered their entire existence. The difference between the hands that gave alms and the ones that brought healing was the touch of the Holy Spirit.

> *Wonder is born in encounter but released through engagement*

Peter and John both saw him, but not as they'd seen him before. They had fresh eyes because they had been in a fresh Wind.

WONDER ATTRACTS PEOPLE WHO NEED WONDERS

Luke was a master of details, and this account is no different. Something attracted the lame man's attention to Peter & John in particular.

Now this was a busy place. There were many people passing through every moment. The idea that this man noticed Peter and John is akin to picking out two strangers in the middle of a crowded shopping mall.

Something in these two fishermen made something in this helpless lame man believe something special was about to happen. You see it in his reaction. *"He saw...he asked..."*[4]

> *People living in wonder create thirst in people who need wonders*

I am convinced this prompted Peter's statement some years later when in his Apostolic letter he wrote, *"Always be prepared to give an answer to everyone who asks you to give the reason for the hope that you have."*[5]

We need answers when we have questions. We ask questions when our interest is piqued.

So the crippled beggar asked for money. It's what he thought he needed. Peter and John gave him healing because that's what he really needed.

Something told them that something in them could handle whatever was before them. *"Look at us"*[6] is a strange demand for such unimpressive people as these two blue-collared fishermen. But these newly baptized preachers demanded his attention because they had something to show him. The man gave them his attention, *"expecting to receive."*[7]

Walk in wonder and you'll create expectation wherever you go. That's as it should be. Believers in Jesus owe the world answered prayers—Heaven's solutions to earth's problems.

The flip side of that coin is if the Church demands the world's attention, we better have something supernatural to give them when we get it. It thrills Jesus when we live in a way that causes those around us to take notice. But what they need to notice is that we have been with Him. Anything less leaves all parties unimpressed!

WONDER SEES IMPOSSIBLE WITH HEAVEN'S EYES

Peter's approach went something like this. "What I had the last time you saw me won't do you any good. But what I have now will change your life!" It was his declaration of dependence. Only God could provide the evidence to underwrite Peter's confidence. Either Holy Spirit moved in that moment, or these fishermen would get skunked!

Surely in that instant, the specific promises Jesus had tucked into their hearts came rushing back. In fact, it was John who would record them.

- *"I will do whatever you ask **in my name**, so that the Father may be glorified in the Son. You may ask me for anything **in my name**, and I will do it."*[8]
- *"Whatever you ask **in my name** the Father will give you."*[9]
- *"In that day you will ask **in my name**."*[10]
- *"Very truly I tell you, my Father will give you whatever you ask **in my name**. Until now you have not asked for anything **in my name**. Ask and you will receive, and your joy will be complete."*[11]

But Mark, Peter's associate, captured it best. *"And these signs will accompany those who believe: **In my name** they will drive out demons; they will speak in new tongues; they will pick up snakes with their hands; and when they drink deadly poison, it will not hurt them at all; they will place their hands on sick people, and they will get well."*[12]

So the Disciples pulled the only trump card they held. *"**In the name of Jesus Christ of Nazareth, walk.**"*[13]

Peter then engaged in a transaction of defiance. By reaching out his hand, he got close enough to make a difference. When he helped the man up, he got involved enough to make a sacrifice. But then came the healing. Peter got to see God up close and personal.

What happened next was nothing less than a wonder. The man who had never taken a step, *"jumped to his feet and began to walk. Then he went with them into the temple courts, walking and jumping, and praising God."*[14]

> ## The lame man became a wonder-walker!

That's how it works.

When we live in wonder, God releases wonders. That Wonder causes witness. *"When all the people saw him walking and praising God, they recognized him as the same man who used to sit begging at the temple gate called Beautiful…"* That witness creates more Wonder. *"They were filled with wonder and amazement at what had happened to him."*[15]

Wonder is cyclical. Our wonder inspires God to do wonders. God's wonders generate more wonder.

There is nothing better than being caught in that vortex.

SET UP

"The things that matter most must never be
at the mercy of the things that matter least."
~Johann Volfgang von Goethe

When we walk in wonder, we become enemies of anything that robs God of His dream in us or in others. It literally turns our stomach to be in an atmosphere where God's heart is misrepresented or His purpose distorted. Mature wonder understands that anything not increasing the glory of God is short-sighted or blind.

Wonder is a Kingdom mindset where we've learned to think from Heaven to Earth. This mindset Incontrovertibly and intractably opposes the thinking of an idolatrous culture.

> "I have nothing but hatred for them;
> I count them my enemies."
> ~Psalm 139:22

The psyche of our contemporary culture is controlled by what I've termed "substitute transcendencies." People frantically pursue transcendent experiences because they can't escape that God made humans for more but we are living for less. Our spirits will not tolerate the tradeoff.

Society has concocted many surrogates to satisfy the part of us made for transcendence. There are obvious ones: mind-altering substances, metaphysical experiences, sexual deviations. But there are also subtle forms of escape that have risen in popularity—everything from obsessive gaming, online gambling, adventure seeking, thrill rides, money seeking, meme stocks and cryptocurrencies.

We basically chase anything that alters the reality we're living and provides a temporary sense that we are living for more. But those wells run dry so fast.

If we are honest about this phenomenon, it is just a form of false worship—misapplied affection. Adoration of something or someone who doesn't deserve it. "Idolatry" is the Bible's old-fashioned word for it. Seeking God-experiences outside of God-relationship. The ultimate deepfakery.

> *The fearful thing is*
> *what we worship we become*

Perhaps the greatest challenge we face as Jesus-followers is around "mindset"—the attention posture that sets the trajectory of life.

We're driven again to what Jesus said, *"Unless you change and become like a little child you cannot see the Kingdom of Heaven."*[1] His point is simple, the truth inescapable. To see what is really going on in the world, we need the open and creative imagination of a little child. We must see things differently.

Cancel culture fights this recalibration of mind aggressively. A systematic effort to shape mindset through traditional and social media, education, popular opinion has been largely successful. This creates a groupthink designed to force ideas through the sieve of a philosophy absent anything absolute—especially God.

Now it's not that the world asks us to abandon belief in God. Culture doesn't mind a god as long as it looks like them. In fact, society at large is constantly working to create a god in its own image. What it will not tolerate is when we propose a God who does not look like us and determine our lifestyle based on that perception. Here's the dilemma in which this contemporary mindset sets us.

We think what we think is what God thinks. But what God really thinks isn't what we think He thinks at all. That leaves us with a choice. We can cling to what we think He should think and miss what He really thinks. Or we can *unthink* what we think He should think and discover what He actually thinks, which we honestly didn't think He would ever think at all.

Read that again. Slowly.

The remedy for this generally accepted outlook of secularism is to rethink our thinking until the mind of Christ becomes our plumb line. Only then can we comprehend our reality as He does.

Paul unpacked this in a letter to a really smart church struggling to adjust their mind to the thoughts of God. *"Since, then, you have been raised with Christ,* **set your hearts** *on things above, where Christ is, seated at the right hand of God.* **Set your minds** *on things above, not on earthly things. For you died, and your life is now hidden with Christ in God. When Christ, who is your life, appears, then you also will appear with him in glory."*[2]

He instructs his friends that both the affections (heart) and thinking (mind) need to be set "up." Above, where Jesus is. Our passion and perspective are from Heaven to earth, not earth to Heaven.

"Since you have been raised with Christ." The opening volley confronts us with a spiritual reality from which we all operate.

In a world upside down to God's reality
we are now right-side-up

Eugene Peterson vividly captures this lofty idea in the Message. *"Pursue the things over which Christ presides. Don't shuffle along, eyes to the ground, absorbed with the things right in front of you.* **Look up** *and be alert to what is going on around Christ—that's where the action is.* **See things from his perspective."**

Paul writes to the sister church in Ephesus, *"God raised us up with Christ and* **seated us with him in the heavenly realms in Christ Jesus,** *in order that in the coming ages he might show the incomparable riches of his grace, expressed in his kindness to us in Christ Jesus. For it is by grace you have been saved, through faith—and this is not from yourselves, it is the gift of God— not by works, so that no one can boast. For we are God's handiwork, created in Christ Jesus to do good works, which God prepared in advance for us to do."*[3]

That is our *real reality*. We live our entire lives becoming what we already are. Grace has positioned us in Christ at the right hand of God—already set into Heaven. This explains why Jesus taught us to pray, *"Let your Kingdom come, let your will be done on earth as it is in heaven.*"[4] It's rational in the Kingdom to think and pray from above.

What does it take in life as it is to think from heaven to earth? Paul gives us two simple—I didn't say easy—things to do.

SET YOUR PASSION

Passion is what you seek based on what you love. When the Apostle demands, *"set your affections,"* he is referring to matters of the heart. This is an action of attention and ambition. There is nothing automatic about it.

In fact, the verb tense is something like this, *"Seek & keep on seeking."* It's yearning for life here to be like it is above. The word is strong enough to be translated, *"envy Heaven."* J. B. Phillips renders the phrase, *"Give your heart to the heavenly things."* Jesus must become the preoccupation of our longings.

> *We are called to choose what we want most over what we want now*

But the direction of affection isn't enough. Paul also commands, *"set your mind."* Fill your thoughts with Heavenly realities; don't let your ambition be earth bound. Make it the aim and habit of your mind to think like Jesus. This powerful word picture has to do with reining in the mind like a wild horse.

Set your thinking means you direct your mind until you understand what you're thinking about from the divine perspective. Of course, there will always be fog in the picture. *"For now [in this time of imperfection] we see in a mirror dimly [a blurred reflection, a riddle, an enigma]."*[5]

We constantly must reset the focus of mind and heart because they keep getting knocked out of focus by unanswered questions, disappointments, loss and pain. Set and keep on setting—always adjusting the scope of earth to the target of Heaven.

When you fix your affection on things above because you've set your mind there, you quickly understand the only things worth pursuing are *up*.

SET YOUR PERSPECTIVE

Perspective is how you see based on Who you love. Paul sets the direction of our affections and thinking *"up."* Essentially, he commands us to *think up*. The phrase, *"on things above,"* is best translated *"the upper."* The intrigue of this statement lies in this: it does not mean to *look up*, but to look *from up*.

We can't understand this world correctly by looking at it from the natural perspective. We will not find hope if we simply try to look up from whatever circumstances we are under. Instead, we look from the place where Christ now sits.

So what does that look like?

First, you must **start with a new ending.** We live from victory. Christ is already the *seated* reigning King. *Above* is the place where Jesus sits in authority.[6] He sat down and remains seated to this moment. He took His place and will not relinquish it.

> *Jesus sat down and
> He isn't going anywhere*

"Seated at the right hand of God," is a phrase reserved exclusively for Jesus that occurs at least 11 times in the New Testament.[7] He sits wearing the Name above every name (Phil 2). Jesus reigns over an ever-expanding, ever-increasing, ever-progressing Kingdom.

That reign of triumph is where we think from!

Next, we must **stand in a new place.** We live from identity. Paul states an accomplished fact: *"you died."* I'd like to add, stop resurrecting yourself!! Quit falling back into old mindsets and life-choices. You are dead. You have a new life—His life. Resurrection life.

And that life is *"hidden with Christ in God."* I love that word *"hidden."* It is the Greek word from which we get "encrypted." God encrypts the transcendence He built you for in Jesus. And this Jesus told us we hold *"the Keys of the Kingdom."*[8]

Believers have the encryption key to unlock what is really happening behind the scenes of all we see.

Which means we must also *seize a new reality.* We live from destiny. *"When Christ, who is your life, appears, then you also will appear with him in glory."* This is our destination. But it also defines our destiny. Paul encourages us to grow up into what we're made for.

Look at Jesus until we look like Jesus.

Paul says when Jesus appears (both now and ultimately at the Second Coming) we also *"appear."* This word refers to our unfiltered shining so people can see what was hidden. Jesus desires our thinking to be so radical that it is undeniably apparent to those around us that we belong to Him.

Jesus wants to go public in you and me!

When He goes public in us, we display who we were made to be. Brian Simmons expresses it this way in the Passion Translation, *"And as Christ himself is seen for who he really is, who you really are will also be revealed, for you are now one with him in his glory!"* Eugene Peterson says it this way, *"When Christ (your real life, remember) shows up again on this earth, you'll show up, too—the real you, the glorious you."*

Jesus is more accurately represented NOW in the earth when we live from the "up" mindset. But real life demands we also acknowledge, we will only be perfectly formed like Him when He returns.[9]

When Jesus calls "that's a wrap" on His-story, not only will He be seen, but all the hidden work of His Kingdom will finally surface. It will shock Hell, thrill Heaven and surprise Earth when His beautiful Bride is unveiled.

Wonder is that *"up"* mindset. It's when our lives are governed not by what is seen in the limited landscape of the earthly perspective, but in the limitless panorama of Heaven's point of view.

OPEN SOURCE

"We are in a risky business…
the conquest of space is worth the risk of life."
~Gus Grissom

It is a hard reality, but the same spiritual and emotional tools which are necessary for us to face life's aches are also essential to feel life's awe. You can't have one without the other.

It's kind of like my fingertips after playing guitar for a while. I am grateful that callouses form to protect me from the pain of the sharp metal strings. But those same callouses prevent me from feeling the soft beauty of my wife's satin blouse or silky skin.

> "Search me, God, and know my heart;
> test me and know my anxious thoughts."
> ~Psalm 139:23

Self-protective defense mechanisms that limit vulnerability strangle intimacy. Transparency is the single trait that opens your heart to be known, embraced and loved with no airbrushed unreality. It is the most important prerequisite to wonder.

I think it's fascinating that David begins this powerfully reflective Psalm 139 by saying, *"You have searched me and know me."* He then ends it the same way. He's saying to God, "do it again."[1] David understood that being open to the Lord was the only way he could continually walk in wonder.

> *The risk of being exposed was worth the reward of being known*

One summer our soccer-star grandson, Mikey, was involved in a soccer camp while he stayed at our home. When the coach had the young players all primed and ready for battle, he would ask them, "Are you ready!?" Their enthusiastic response was, "I was born ready, coach!" I can't count the number of times I heard that in response to my "are you ready" moments that summer!

That declaration works great for soccer, but the truth in life is we weren't born ready. Getting and staying ready demands effort and requires openness.

Vulnerability—living with an open heart of wonder—demands a level of trust that can only be built on the goodness of God. Jesus painted beautiful pictures of that goodness for his often-befuddled friends.

Luke records them like this:[2]

- *"Consider the ravens: They do not sow or reap, they have no storeroom or barn; yet God feeds them... how much more valuable you are than birds!"*
- *"Consider how the wild flowers grow. They do not labor or spin. Yet I tell you, not even Solomon in all his splendor was dressed like one of these. If that is how God clothes the grass of the field...how much more will he clothe you!"*

These promises of provision and favor are heartwarming and faith building. Yet, the challenges Jesus interlaced with them should give us pause.[3]

- *"Do not set your heart on what you will eat or drink; do not worry about it. Seek his kingdom, and these things will be given to you as well."*
- *"Provide...treasure in heaven that will never fail, where no thief comes near and no moth destroys. For where your treasure is, there your heart will be also."*

"Seek first..." and *"Lay up treasures"* both involve a quality of surrender that stretch faith and strain hope. Seeking presupposes a tension between what I have and what I'm looking for. It traffics in the paradoxical space between life as it is and life as it should be.

The Psalmist pictures this tension vividly. A deer panting for water; a parched soul languishing in a desert; the heart and flesh that cries with longing.[4] The ache of hope and expectation is keen in the space of waiting. But such is the construct of seeking.

We sweat when we seek

The food and clothes in Jesus' promise aren't so we can rest comfortably. They're there to help us run uncomfortably. The conundrum is: how do we keep seeking, believing, hoping and expecting in seasons of delay? How do we stay open when it feels so much safer to shut down?

In Luke's account, Jesus follows His promises with a story detailing the uneasiness of life at the Kingdom edge. The parable contains simple wisdom about living vulnerably open to God.

> *"Be dressed ready for service and keep your lamps burning, like servants waiting for their master to return from a wedding banquet, so that when he comes and knocks they can immediately open the door for him. It will be good for those servants whose master finds them watching when he comes. Truly I tell you, he will dress himself to serve, will have them recline at the table and will come and wait on them. It will be good for those servants whose master finds them ready, even if he comes in the middle of the night or toward daybreak. But understand this: If the owner of the house had known at what hour the thief was coming, he would not have let his house be broken into. You also must be ready, because the Son of Man will come at an hour when you do not expect him."[5]*

This Parable isn't just about end times. It's about our times. It's about any time you chase His heart or seek His hand. Any moment when you stand at the precipice of hope.

Jesus had a name for this kind of living: *"life more abundant."*[6] Life with the stops pulled out! For Him, being *"ready"* equaled alive living. There is a vast difference between being alive and alive living. Everyone who breathes is alive. But not everyone who is alive is living. We are called to live on the ragged edge where we're always ready for God to move.

Jesus' attitude toward this abundant life was clear and frank.

His parable left me with a question. Why use the metaphor *"dressed and ready?"* Perhaps the logic is something like this. In the Kingdom there is always somewhere to go and something to do! Like the night of the Old Testament Passover in Egypt. The Jews were told to wear sandals and coats with bags packed. God would move suddenly and they had to be ready to go.

Jesus' story drafts the blueprints of living ready, with an open heart under an open Heaven.

Be Open To Presence

Biblical waiting has two distinct flavors. Waiting in anticipation and serving in action. Either form has a single aim. Prepare for Presence.

> *"Like servants waiting for their master to return from a wedding banquet, so that when he comes and knocks they can immediately open the door for him."*[7]

Wait in anticipation and work with energy because our Master is coming. We're not just talking second coming here. Presence is the context for daily existence.

He's pointing out what we actually long for as human beings. Our impatient ache is for Him—not what He does or gives. We long for a Person. We seek Presence. The hunger so poorly sated by a culture without a clue is not for the stuff or sensations of time. The ache is for eternity. We hunger for Heaven. We clam up and close up because we consume what we were never made to digest.

The *"ready"* of this story is about vulnerable openness to His intimate intrusions. We stay alert so when He *"knocks"* we *"immediately open the door."* This Jesus who *"stands at the door and knocks,"* can walk through walls, but He prefers to enter doors willingly opened.

Be Open For More

> *"It will be good for those servants whose master finds them watching when he comes. Truly I tell you, he will dress himself to serve, will have them recline at the table and will come and wait on them. It will*

be good for those servants whose master finds them ready, even if he comes in the middle of the night or toward daybreak."[8]

Jesus sees us waiting and is drawn into it. He loves finding people who are finding Him. The Father's heart seeks seekers. God chases chasers.

- *"Yet a time is coming and has now come when the true worshipers will worship the Father in the Spirit and in truth, for they are the kind of worshipers the Father seeks."*[9]
- *"For the eyes of the Lord run to and fro throughout the whole earth, to show Himself strong on behalf of those whose heart is loyal to Him."*[10]
- *"Then you will call on me and come and pray to me and I will listen to you. You will seek me and find me when you seek me with all your heart. I will be found by you, declares the LORD."*[11]

Jesus says it's *"good"* when He finds seekers. What makes it good?

A seeking heart moves His hand

Something about the movement of your heart toward His moves God toward you. *"Move your heart closer and closer to God, and he will come even closer to you."*[12] Like the Prodigal Father in Jesus' famous story, God is always itching to run off the porch and catch you mid-repentance.

So much so that in this parable, the Master *"will dress himself to serve, will have them recline at the table and will come and wait on them."* The King will enter your space and get his hands dirty helping you.

What a wonder!

Be Open To Fight

"But understand this: If the owner of the house had known at what hour the thief was coming, he would not have let his house be broken into."[13]

Jesus says there is an existential threat against His house. That peril motivates the awakened disciple to live ready. There is a battle. We live in a war zone.

Casualties are a constant reality. But the enemy doesn't get to pillage uncontested. There might be a fight, but the contest has been called!

Wonder is not out-of-touch to the warfare raging around the ones chasing Father's heart. Here is a stark truth wonder never forgets.

> *We are writing a love song in a war zone*

Wisdom gained in the waiting and refined by the watching prepares us for battle.

Be Open To Surprise

We live in constant anticipation because Kingdom Come is also Kingdom Coming! There's always more.

> *"You also must be ready, because the Son of Man will come at an hour when you do not expect him."*[14]

In the kingdom, we must be ready for anything. God always and forever is Master of the unexpected.. He has a habit of moving in *"suddenlies"*—moments when life unexplainably changes because God unexpectedly shows up. He's a big God and full of surprises. We never know when they're coming.

The adventure of this chase is that we can find ourselves at any moment in a *suddenly* that shifts the atmosphere and changes the outcome of our deepest longings. Ready clings to moment miracles until momentous miracles come.

It's the mystery in our history that shapes our destiny.

ONE WAY

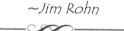

"It is the set of the sails, not the direction of the wind, that determines which way we will go."
~Jim Rohn

The path into Wonder is as simple as surrender. David closes this potent Psalm with words that under the surface are chock-full of significance.

He stands emotionally naked before God—utterly vulnerable. The request is frighteningly loaded. "God, look in the deepest part of me and see if there is anything that offends you…anything that is less than your best." He uses the description *"wicked way"* to sum up that which He wants God to root out.

The word translated *"way"* is the same one used in Solomon's famous axiom, *"Train up a child in the way he should go and when he is old he will not depart from it."*[1] It's best rendered *"bent."* The Psalmist is asking God for raw honesty. Dig deep and find any bent toward wickedness and straighten it out.

Here is a prayer of vulnerable surrender. The expression of man in pursuit of the heart of God. He would settle for nothing less.

> "See if there is any offensive way in me, and lead me in the way everlasting."
> ~Psalm 139:24

Modern culture poo-poos any suggestion that surrender is a good thing. Instead, we live by adages like "never give up" and "fight to the finish." In many situations, that kind of courage is admirable. But not if you're protecting things that are compromising your character or sabotaging your destiny.

Anyone chasing the heart of God wants Him to search the caverns of the soul for anything undermining created purpose.

Such surrender is the height of courage. Transparency with God puts us in a position for Him to transform us into carriers of His presence and conduits of His power. With our insides "straightened out," we can walk into a place where God can safely blow our minds.

Surrender is the posture of wonder

Her name was Ruth.[2] Her life is a poignant picture of the incredible benefits of Godly surrender. She is one of those characters whose bit part in the Story of Redemption turns into a leading role. Let's look at her early biography.

Ruth was a *"Moabitess."* Simply put, she was an outsider to the nation of Israel and normally would have been unwelcome at any Jewish party. But hunger overcomes prejudice every time. There was a famine in Israel that led a woman to move her family to Moab simply to survive.

Naomi, Elimelek and their sons relocated out of desperation. They lived away from home for a very long time. The patriarch died, the boys grew up and at marrying age, found brides among the Moabites because they were the only prospects. Not the first choice of an Israelite, but needs must.

One son married Orpah, the other married Ruth. Then tragedy struck. Both Mahlon and Kilion died, leaving three widows to fend for themselves. In ancient society, this was a grim picture.

Naomi soon realized moving home was her only option to find family and get aid. The bitter, disappointed woman set out with widowed daughters-in-law in tow. Along the way, the older widow realized her Moabite lasses would not find favorable prospects for marriage and family among Jewish men. She did all she could to get them to turn back to Moab for a fresh start. Orpah saw the logic and reluctantly returned.

But something in Ruth knew her future was ahead of her, not behind. She understood her history did not need to determine her destiny. So she bound herself to Naomi using some of the most profound words in Scripture. *"Where you go I will go, and where you stay I will stay. Your people will be my people and your God my God. Where you die I will die, and there I will be buried."*[3]

Such is the heart of surrender. This is hope's last stand. Ruth displayed an attitude of ultimate trust and absolute commitment. She positioned herself where only God could create the future for which she desperately hoped.

Ruth saw the risk of going forward was far less than the risk of going back. She entered her future holding onto a depressed mother-in-law in a land where she was a second-class citizen who would always play second fiddle. Not pretty, but something told her a preferable future lay there.

She lost it all because she wanted more

This Moabite widow quickly learned that when you assume the posture of surrender, you untie the hands of God. The breathtaking story is a fairy tale written in Heaven but played out on earth.

Enter Boaz. The kinsman redeemer—the one with the right and ability to change everything not only for Ruth but by inference, Naomi. Through a series of miracles, Ruth arrives at a moment where seizing her destiny, even at substantial risk, is the absolute best option.

Ruth was living under Boaz' blessing. But this blessing was not all she was after. She wanted him. She wanted his heart. His presence in her life and the potential that lay in that relationship were worth more than any blessing he could bestow.

Naomi unwittingly gives Ruth the steps of true surrender. She instructs Ruth to wash, put on perfume and dress well. Go secretly and wait for the right opportunity. *"Lie at his feet to let him know that you are available to him for marriage. Then wait and see what he says. He'll tell you what to do."*[4]

What a picture of surrender! She didn't care how it looked to others. She knew being at his feet was the safest place on earth.
- *Lie at his feet*—the humble posture of vulnerable submission.
- *Lift the cover*—a simple request for the covering of covenant.
- *Let him know you are available*—expose your heart to Him.

Ruth was not trying to seduce him but to display the value she placed on Him. She was expressing the greatest possible trust in him. By her action, Ruth showed her desire for Boaz and her willingness to marry him.

This was no small request. The question was not whether he loved her, but whether he wanted to take on the responsibility. Did Boaz think she was worth it? After all, he would not inherit what had belonged to her husband, that would go to any children they produced. He was taking on a responsibility that had no tangible benefits for him except her presence and affection.

But that was enough for him. It was more than enough for her.

Surrender is both a dangerous safe thing and a safe dangerous thing. It involves giving God all you are and have—nothing held back; nothing in reserve. Absolutely abandoned to His will with total trust in His character.

Boaz lived up to Ruth's trust. The risk she'd taken and the commitment she'd made moved him deeply. Her fearless trust planted a flag in His heart. He provided her with intimacy, restored her identity and changed her destiny. The outcast found her influence; the outsider found her home. Her surrender released fruitfulness—they had a son. That son restored Grandma Naomi's heart as well.

This was God-sized wonder

Fast forward a couple generations and she's blessed with a great-grandson named David of Bethlehem. Centuries later, she had a 30th-generation grand name Jesus of Nazareth. Because Ruth risked surrender, she walked in wonder.

A *big* message in a *short* story.

Ruth displays how God works wonders through the simple stories of average people. He's constructing a grand story from small, seemingly inconsequential stories of everyday people. God intentionally placed Ruth's story in the storyline of Scripture at the end of one epoch (the Old Testament Patriarchs) and the beginning of a larger one (the Kings). Ruth's inclusion in the flow of Old Testament history is an exclamation point to the confession, "God Almighty is a wonder-worker!"

I love how David closes this very personal Psalm 139 by asking God to lead him into the way everlasting. That word *"lead"*[5] is the picture of an instructor taking the lead in a dance. David puts himself in the Father's arms and asks Him to teach him the dance of Heaven. His choreographer is the Lord of the dance and David's cry is, "Teach me the dance of wonder!"

Peter picks up the theme in the New Testament when he deliberately chooses a dance term to illustrate how God brings us each into the Kingdom. *"As a result (of walking with Jesus), the kingdom's gates will open wide to you as God choreographs your triumphant entrance into the eternal kingdom of our Lord and Savior, Jesus the Messiah."*[6]

The Greek term for bringing us into the Kingdom is *epichorēgeo*. Can you hear it—choreography? Most translations use words to the effect of *"richly provide."* Brian Simmons gets it right.

God choreographs our entrance into the Kingdom.

When our daughter Lauren was small, she loved to stand on my shoes and dance with me at any party we attended. We moved as one because she was literally standing on my feet—effortlessly walking in my steps. Whenever I moved, wherever I moved, she synchronized perfectly. Simply surrendered to my choreography.

Much like that, our walk of wonder is simply a dance where we stand on the pierced feet of the One who created the steps.

My heart for you is so well expressed in the lyrics of a hit country song recorded by Lee Ann Womack.

> I hope you never lose your sense of wonder
> You get your fill to eat, but always keep that hunger
> May you never take one single breath for granted
> God forbid love ever leave you empty-handed
>
> And when you get the choice to sit it out or dance…
> I hope you dance![7]

WALKING IN WONDER

———————— ⚜ ————————

Every year the season of Advent (Christmas for many of you) moves my heart deeply. I am a self-confessed Advent Junkie.[1] I love everything about the season and the miracle expressed so simply by John the Beloved.

> *"The Word became flesh and pitched His tent among us, and we saw His glory."*[2]

I never get tired of the truth that the God of the Universe came to be our next-door neighbor. So close he could sneak in as a houseguest sipping coffee in his pajamas, watching Jeopardy in a recliner or playing football with the kids in the backyard.

God playing divine show and tell in time and space.

Jesus came so we can see what God looked like when He looked like us. But Jesus also came so we can see what we look like when we look like God. His highest purpose was to show us how our address could look like His address. His prayer for it was *"Kingdom of God, come! Will of God, be done! On earth as it is in Heaven."*[3]

During Advent 2021, I had an unprecedented and unparalleled experience. Not being particularly "prophetic," I've had almost no night dreams I could unequivocally blame on God. But on December 8, 2021 at three a.m., I had just such a dream. I got out of bed and wrote it down as accurately as I could to the nearly crystal-clear vision I'd seen and heard.

I share it here because it so beautifully portrays this walk of wonder I've tried to describe in the preceding pages. May it fuel you on this adventure of chasing our Father's heart.

THE DREAM

I was staying at an old-school motel on a nearby beach. It was one of those nondescript, retro single-story 60's motels. I answered a knock at the door. A young man smiled and said, "I've come to take you to Heaven. Do you want to go?" I figured it must be my time to go, so with no fear I gladly said, "Yes!"

The guest took my hand and we began to walk. We moved through what seemed to be one of those TV movie dissolves where everything goes blurry and then you emerge in a new place. But as we emerged, we were simply standing outside the door of my hotel room.

I turned to my new friend and said, "I thought I was going to Heaven." He replied, "You did." I questioningly responded, " But this is where we just were." And he said, "Well what did you expect?" That's when I asked disappointedly, "If this is Heaven and it's just like where I was, what's the difference?" He smiled and replied, "You'll see."

We started walking down the sidewalk along the stretch of highway A1A in front of the motel, passing all the attendant surf shops and tourist traps.

Coming toward us was a stream of people, some I knew, some I didn't. Many were friends. A few were people I knew had feelings against me. Others were people whose faces I didn't know but who had obvious conditions of illness. Some limping, others with facial deformities, a few in wheelchairs. One thing I noticed, they were all conditions representing people I had seen and prayed for in weeks before the dream.

As they neared us, it was as if they passed through some sort of force-field radiating dozens of feet in front of me. As each passed through, they were transformed so I saw them as they would be in Heaven. When it was a believing friend or family member, not a lot changed. I could just tell we had both lost the limitations of earth and were connecting in the perfection of Heaven.

But then, one of the people with ought against me walked into that zone and everything changed. The angry scowl became a smile, the ugly look disappeared. There was a hug and a joyous greeting, as if nothing ever stood between us. Heaven had changed it all. My young guide unexplainably seemed to know everyone and was really pleased at the reunions.

As we resumed our walk, those with the conditions of brokenness passed into the holy space in which I was walking. As the limping person passed through, the leg was completely healed and he immediately walked with a spring in the step. The person with severe deformity passed through and the grotesque distortion disappeared, and I saw them for the first time without it. Perfect and whole. The most dramatic image was a man in a wheelchair. As he rolled into the zone, he rose out of the chair and walked perfectly upright—restored and well.

I turned to my guide and said, "I get it now! Heaven is a place much like we live in now but with none of the physical, emotional, relational and spiritual baggage I experience every day. It isn't puffy clouds and harps; it is life very much as we know it now but free of sin and evil. A new earth like the one we have, but the way God made it in the beginning."

A huge grin ripped across His face and he blurted out, "You got it, Dude!!"

Then he continued. "That isn't all. There is so much more I want to tell you. The reason I let you see Heaven in your current construct is not only to show you what Heaven is going to be like, but to remind you that when I came, I came to bring Heaven into the very context you live NOW."

That's when I realized my guest and guide was Jesus. I didn't get it before because He literally looked and sounded like some local surfer! He deepened his explanation.

"When I came in Bethlehem and burst into earth through my mother Mary's womb, I poked a hole in the membrane between Heaven and earth." He looked at me and smiled a mischievous smile, then winked and said, "Heaven sprang a leak!"

He talked me through His life. It reminded me of two guys on a road to a town called Emmaus. "I lived what you just saw. As people got near me, My presence changed them to become more like what they will be in Heaven. At first it was only a little, but Heaven was breaking in. At the Temple when I was 12, the leaders saw a bit of Heaven on earth. So did the guests at the wedding where I did the wine thing. But as I encountered more of the pain of my broken world, the tear in the Heavens got bigger as more of what exists there invaded what is here.

At my baptism, the hole ripped further as the Spirit burst through and rested on me. With each miracle, the heavenly pressure on that tear increased. Then at Golgotha, as the Heavens shook, that rip grew larger. It nearly burst completely when I rose from the grave. Even a few of my friends snuck out of their graves that day and walked around Jerusalem. Heaven was breaking in big time.

At my departure, my friends looked up to see a wide-open Heaven receive me. That pinprick had become a massive open door. Now Heaven was leaking profusely.

But the real flood really started on the Day of Pentecost. That membrane of separation could no longer hold the pressure of Heaven's weight. My Spirit rushed in on my people and a raging flood of life released and became unstoppable."

That's when He looked at me and it became so personal as he said, "I know you love Advent. But you need to remember, when I came in flesh, that incarnation was not a consummation, it was an initiation. An invitation. The reason I showed you Heaven on A1A is that what I want most is not for you to come to Heaven. It is for Heaven to come through you. Here. Now.

What you saw is what I came for. To bring Heaven to earth until I bring earth to Heaven."[4]

ACKNOWLEDGEMENTS

I always want to acknowledge my wife of over 42 years. Dianne has walked in wonder through some of the darkest and most difficult times imaginable. She lives transfixed on Jesus' face and is nothing short of a worship animal! Her obsession with Holy Spirit causes all who know her to wonder how to wonder like that! Thank you, Babe, for loving me and teaching me that there's no one quite like Jesus.

My growing tribe of children and grandchildren. Their love, forgiveness and endurance have shaped so much of what I've learned about living for Jesus. Watching their journeys has left me breathless and built my wonder at the King and His Kingdom. I am infinitely richer and truly honored being Dad and Papa.

So grateful for my siblings, Hal, Kathy, Carla and Ron; and siblings-in-law, Grace, Al, Barry, Theresa, Bill and Pete. Your love has buoyed me through the years. How you've filled my wonder tank!

My big sister, Kathy. As always, thanks for massaging these words into something that makes sense. You have given and cheered so hard for me to get my words into books.

My friends, Steve, Cathy, John, Susan, Saundra, Al, Brad, Lita, Bee, Missy, Tom, David, Caron...and so many more. The experience of walking out restoration in the company of these who refused to stop believing in me has meant authentic experience of *"on earth as in heaven."*

Those who have pastored me, Mack & Alyson Tucker, Jeff & Ann Hoy, Roger & Angel Hackenberg, Tim & Kelly Franklin. Shepherds who have modeled for me and guided their flock in the wonderful grace of the Lord Jesus.

ABOUT THE AUTHOR

About the Author
Michael W. Thompson

Michael cut his teeth on church pews. He grew up in a tight-knit pastor's home and then spent 20 years of his professional life as a worship leader and senior pastor. However, ministry success was derailed by moral failure that painfully altered the trajectory of his life, family and ministry.

But God had not finished. In extravagant grace, He has restored Michael and Dianne. Their rescued marriage and rebuilt family are a living message of hope and healing for the Body of Christ.

This journey birthed an unquenchable passion: to see *life as it is* transformed into *life as it should be.* You *feel* this fire in his books. He and Dianne have made it their singular pursuit to discover the design, desire and delight of the Father.

Spending the last 20 years in the marketplace has also given him a unique perspective. Knitting together the distinct realms of church and commerce results in Michael's rather visceral understanding of Kingdom living.

Michael and Dianne have been married over 40 years. They have three adult children who, with their loves have given them a growing brood of grandchildren.

Learn more at www.MichaelWThompson.com

BOOKS

Tipping The Scales: *Harness Your Pain to Empower Your Prayer*

Nothing is more important than hearing God when you need Him most. It's a matter of life and death to talk honestly with God about the stuff that's killing you. Life gets hard so prayer must get real. Prayer that is forged in the fire of life's crucible drops from the head to the heart. Praying from your heart moves God's.

"This book leaks grace from every page. The real kind. The empowering kind. The hope-filled kind. Grace. Tipping the Scales is truly a godsend." –Bill Johnson, Bethel Church

Swapping Stories: *Bible Backstories That Shape Our Stories To Make HIStory*

If we are honest, most of us would prefer to change places—swap stories—with at least one person we know. The story God is writing in the lives of those around us can seem so much more compelling, appealing or important than our own. Ours is messier.

We look regretfully at yesterday and wonder "what is" or apprehensively at today and question "what good?" Perhaps uneasily at tomorrow and muse "what for?"

But God sees our stories differently! The Bible proves that God makes History through people just like you.

Print & Ebooks

Available at MichaelWThompson.com or Amazon

Everyday Eternity: *Surprised By God In The Routines Of Life*

Hidden in the daily are treasures that bring meaning, joy and significance to life. It's time to regain your childlike sense of awe, excitement and amazement at the beautiful things covertly disguised as normal living. Eternity in the everyday. You'll be amazed what surprises God has slipped under the covers of life as you know it. So blink if you must, but dare to open your eyes wide so you can see the beauty so wonderfully disguised as ordinary.

ScarGazing: *Uncover The Hope Hiding In Your Pain*

Scars are signs of survival. They give silent testimony to stories of healing. Every scar gives visible witness to a heartbreak that has healed. Wounds narrate the tragic saga of what pain leaves behind.

But scars sing the triumphant song of what God creates from the residue. It's why scars are beautiful and why we must study them intimately.

We need the stories they tell.

Print & Ebooks
Available at MichaelWThompson.com or Amazon

OTHER TITLES BY THE AUTHOR

DEVOTIONALS

Lent: **The Last Laugh**

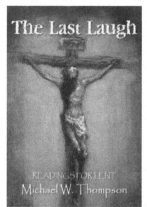

The Author of life flipped the script on power of death. It's never a good idea to laugh at Jesus. He will always challenge what we "know" to be true. Resurrection does that. When angels rolled the stone from His borrowed tomb, the portal between Heaven and earth, between time and eternity opened. Eternity is now permeable. Heaven's door is permanently ajar. The membrane between life and death split like the Temple curtain when Jesus walked out of that grave. He won it all when He exited that mountainside crypt with Hell's keys jangling on His hip. He always gets the last laugh.

Advent: **Veiled In Flesh:** *When God Looked Like Us*

Heaven kissed earth in a Bethlehem stable. Veiled in our flesh, God got too close for comfort. Forget every sappy Christmas movie you've ever seen. There is much more to Christmas than tinsel, trees and too many treats. In a place no king in his right mind would visit, much less allow his son to be born, God came. He inaugurated a single life that would alter every life that followed. The stories of the Season show that God went farther than we could dream, to give us more than we could imagine. Everything changed that one silent night.

Print & Ebooks
Available at MichaelWThompson.com or Amazon

ENDNOTES

Turbulence
1. Psalm 139:14
2. Psalm 139:14, TPT
3. Psalm 145:3-4, TPT
4. 1 Thessalonians 4:18
5. 1 Peter 1:8
6. Philippians 4:4
7. Philippians 3:13
8. Proverbs 3:7, TPT
9. Jeremiah 33:3

A Child's-Eye View
1. Isaiah 9:6
2. Matthew 4:17
3. Mark 10:15/Luke 18:17
4. G.K. Chesterton, All Things Considered
5. Matthew 18:3
6. Psalm 139:1

Authorized Biography
1. Luke 8:26-39, Matthew 9:20-22; Mark 10:46-52; Matthew 26:6-13; Luke 6:6-11
2. Psalm 139:16, MSG
3. Hebrews 12:2
4. Acts 3:15
5. 2 Corinthians 3:3
6. Revelation 12:11
7. Revelation 19:10

Between The Lines
1. Psalm 107:1-2, NIV 2011 edition
2. Ephesians 2:10—TPT
3. Isaiah 61:1-3a
4. Isaiah 61:3b
5. Isaiah 61:4

Plot Twists
1. Robert, Nancy Wolgemuth and Joni Eareckson Tada, *You Can Trust God to Write Your Story: Embracing the Mysteries of Providence* (Chicago: Moody Publishers, 2019), 20.
2. Paul David Trip, *New Morning Mercies*, (Wheaton: Crossway, 2014).
3. Romans 8:28, MSG
4. Hebrews 12:2
5. Psalm 18:20-24, MSG

The Untold Story
1. Psalm 34:18
2. Matthew 5, 7, 9, 13, 18, 20, 21, 22, 25
3. Matthew 13:44
4. Proverbs 25:2
5. Luke 18:17
6. Matthew 6:10
7. Matthew 4:17
8. John 14:12

Headlines & Details
1. Psalm 139:4b-5, TPT
2. 1 Peter 1:17, TPT
3. Genesis 1:1ff

Mystery Writer
1. Neil Armstrong, in a speech to Congress (September 16, 1969).
2. Matthew 11:25
3. Matthew 13:44

What If?
1. Matthew 6:33
2. 1 Thessalonians 4:13
3. Psalm 84:5-7
4. Matthew 5:4
5. MSG Translation

If Only
1. Psalm 23:5a
2. Job 36: 15-13
3. 2 Samuel 4; 9
4. Proverbs 18:24
5. 2 Chron 16:9

Even If
1. Isaiah 6:1a
2. Isaiah 4:2
3. 2 Chron 26
4. John 12:41

If Then
1. Acts 2
2. Genesis 1:1
3. Psalm 90:2
4. Revelation 4:11
5. Isaiah 45:18

6. Hebrews 11:3
7. John 1:3
8. Colossians 1:15
9. Genesis 1:1-2
10. 1 Corinthians 14:33
11. 1 Corinthians 2:7-8
12. John 17:5
13. 1 Peter 1:20
14. Revelation 13:8
15. Matthew 25:34

As If
1. Ecclesiastes 1:2; 12:8
2. Ecclesiastes 1:18, 2:10, 18; 5:7; 10; 8:14; 9:2
3. Ecclesiastes 2:17
4. Song of Songs 2: 16, KJV
5. Song of Songs 6:3, KJV
6. Song of Songs 7:10, KJV
7. Song of Songs 8:12
8. Psalm 33:8, TPT
9. Mark 10:15/Luke 18:17

If Not
1. John 7:17-38
2. Matthew 6:9
3. Galatians 6:9; 2 Thessalonians 3:13
4. Mark 14
5. 2 Kings 4
6. Matthew 7:2
7. Luke 6:38
8. John 15
9. Luke 13:6-9
10. John 15: 2, 5, 8, 16
11. Matthew 11:12-14; 20-26
12. Ezekiel 47:12
13. Revelation 22:1-5

A Stitch In Time
1. Ephesians 3:8-9
2. Ephesians 3:10-11
3. Matthew 6:10
4. Ephesians 2:6
5. Ephesians 3:14
6. Ephesians 3:15-18
7. Ephesians 3:19
8. Ephesians 3:21

Sphere Of Influence
1. Matthew 13:3
2. Matthew 5:13
3. Psalms 80:10-11, TPT
4. Matthew 5:14-16
5. John 9:5; Matthew 5:14
6. Isaiah 60:1-2
7. Psalm 72:3 TPT

Defining Moment
1. The Chosen, copyright © Angel Studios. All rights reserved.
2. Matthew 21:10
3. Luke 2:8
4. John 1:29
5. Matthew 21:6, JBP
6. Matthew 21:7, TPT
7. Matthew 21:9
8. Matthew 21:11
9. Matthew 21:12-13, MSG
10. Matthew 21:14, TPT
11. Matthew 21:15
12. Matthew 21:15, TPT
13. Matthew 21:16
14. Isaiah 40:4

He Knew You When
1. John 11
2. John 11:3
3. John 11:5-6
4. Isaiah 40:31
5. John 11:4
6. John 11:21, 32
7. John 11:35
8. Heb. 4:15-16, TPT

More Than A Dream
1. Joel 2:28
2. Matthew 6:10
3. Luke 2:22-38
4. Proverbs 13:2
5. Matthew 18:3
6. Luke 2:25
7. Luke 2:25
8. Luke 2:36
9. Isaiah 64:1

10. Blessed Assurance, Public Domain
11. Luke 2:27
12. Luke 2:34-35

Lost In Wonder
1. Sky Magazine, Delta Airlines.
2. Exodus 33
3. Psalm 27:4
4. Exodus 33:4
5. Psalm 25:14
6. Exodus 33:13
7. Exodus 33:18

Stark Contrast
1. Stallone, S. (1976) Rocky {Film} USA: United Artists.
2. Genesis 12:2
3. Genesis 21:1-4
4. Romans 4:18
5. MSG
6. TPT
7. Matthew 6:10
8. Romans 4:19, MSG
9. Romans 4:19, MSG
10. Eph 1:18-23
11. Romans 4:18
12. Romans 4:20
13. Romans 4:20b
14. Romans 4:20, JBP
15. Romans 4:20, MSG
16. Isaiah 40:31
17. Heb 6:18-20

Altar Egos
1. Genesis 1:1
2. Genesis 1:26
3. Genesis 2:15-17
4. Genesis 2: 25
5. Genesis 3:1
6. Genesis 3:9
7. Genesis 3:10
8. Genesis 3:11
9. Genesis 3:23-24
10. Dietrich Bonhoeffer, *Life Together*, (London: SCM Press, 2012), Chapter 5.

The Good Fight
1. John 10:10a, TPT

2. John 10:10b, TPT
3. Acts 3
4. Acts 3:3
5. 1 Peter 3:15
6. Acts 3:4
7. Acts 3:5
8. John 14:12-14
9. John 15:16
10. John 16:26a
11. John 16:23b-24
12. Mark 16:17-18
13. Acts 3:6b
14. Acts 3: 8
15. Acts 3:9

Set Up
1. Matthew 18:3
2. Colossians 3:1-4
3. Ephesians 2:6-10
4. Matthew 6:10
5. 1 Corinthians 13:12a, AMP
6. Eph 1:20-21; Romans 8:34
7. Matthew 26:64; Mark 14:62, 16:19; Luke 22:69; Acts 2:34; Ephesians 1:20; Colossians 3:1; Hebrews 1:3, 8:1,
   10:12, 12:2
8. Matthew 16:19
9. 1 John 3:1

Open Source
1. Psalm 139:1, 23
2. Luke 12:22-34
3. Luke 12:31, 33
4. Psalm 42:1-2; 63:1-2; 84:1-2
5. Luke 12:35-40
6. John 10:10b
7. Luke 12:36
8. Luke 12:37-38
9. John 4:23
10. 2 Chronicles 16:9
11. Jeremiah 29:12-14
12. James 4:8, TPT
13. Luke 12:39
14. Luke 12:40

One Way
1. Proverbs 22:6

2. Book of Ruth
3. Ruth 1:16b-17a
4. Ruth 3:4, MSG
5. Psalm 139:24b
6. 2 Peter 1:10b-11, TPT
7. Lee Ann Womack, *I Hope You Dance*, MCA Nashville, 2000; written by Tia Sillers & Mark D. Sanders.

Walking In Wonder

1. See my Advent Devotional, Michael W Thompson, *Veiled in Flesh: When God Looked Like Us*, (Melbourne,
   FL: RevivalLifePress, 2020) available from my website,
   www.MichaelWThompson.com or on Amazon.
2. John 1:14
3. Matthew 6:10, Paraphrase by Jack R. Taylor
4. Originally published as part of a message given to Hope Community Fellowship, Titusville, FL. December 12,
   2021.